BOAT FISHING IN
CORNWALL AND
THE ISLES OF SCILLY

By the same author:
ANGLING IN WEST CORNWALL AND
THE ISLES OF SCILLY

BOAT FISHING AND THE

IN CORNWALL
ISLES OF SCILLY

SID PENDER

DYLLANSOW TRURAN

Dyllansow Truran
Cornish Publications
Trewolsta, Trewirgie, Redruth, Cornwall

Copyright © 1983 Sid Pender

All rights reserved. No part of this publication may be reproduced, stored in a retrieval system, or transmitted, in any form or by any means, electronic, electrostatic, magnetic tape, mechanical, photocopying, recording or otherwise, without permission in writing from the publishers.

First published 1983

*This book is dedicated to
the members of
the Mount's Bay Angling Society*

Printed in Great Britain by A. Wheaton & Co. Ltd, Exeter

ISBN 0 907566-66-9

Foreword

The waters around the coast of Cornwall and the Isles of Scilly offer visiting and local anglers some of the best sea fishing in the British Isles. One sixth of the fish on the British Rod-Caught Record List have been taken from these waters. As the popularity of the sport has increased so has the number of different species brought to the scales. The Cornish Record list shows a total of 65 different species taken from both boat and shore. No other region in the British isles can boast of such a wide variety of sea fish.

This book has been written to answer the perennial questions one hears every summer, 'Where can I go fishing?', 'What fish can I catch?', 'What charter or hire boat facilities are there?' The author is indebted to the secretaries of various local angling clubs and to many Scillonians for their contributions to the text.

The text covers inshore and deep sea fishing around the Cornish coast and the Isles of Scilly with specific reference to the waters fished regularly by the author i.e. Mount's Bay; Sennen Cove and around the Isles of Scilly.

The author comes from a long-established Cornish fishing family and was brought up in Mousehole where his first experience of sea angling was with a handline from the end of the local pier.

After studying at college and teaching in the Oxford area for four years he went to the Isles of Scilly where his four-year stay gave him an intimate knowledge of shore fishing from St.Mary's and the inshore waters between the islands.

On his return to the mainland he became an active member of the Mount's Bay Angling Society and is its present chairman. He is the holder of many club and County records, primarily for inshore species taken from his own dinghies. Many of the junior members of the club have benefited from his experience over the past ten years and to date sixteen County Records, nine Junior and seven Senior, have been set from his own twelve foot dinghies which are kept at Mousehole and Sennen.

During the past year he has been a regular contributor to the 'Sea Angling Monthly' and the weekly national publication 'Angler's Mail'. He has, over the same period, contributed a weekly angling column in the Penzance edition of 'The Cornishman' newspaper.

Contents

List of Illustrations   7

Acknowledgements   8

Introduction   9

1   **Deep Sea Fishing from Cornish Ports**   11

2   **Shark Fishing in Cornish Waters**   16

3   **Inshore Fishing in Cornish Waters**   18

       Estuary Fishing
       Inshore Dinghy Fishing in Penwith Waters
       Inshore Dinghy Fishing from Sennen Cove
       Inshore Boat Fishing for Pollack in West Cornwall
       Record Fish from West Penwith Waters
       Useful Information

4   **Boat Fishing in the Isles of Scilly**   43

       Introduction
       Inshore Boat Fishing in the Isles of Scilly
       Deep Sea Fishing around the Isles of Scilly
       The Former Isles of Scilly Sea Angling Club
       Additional Information for the Isles of Scilly

Index   62

List of Illustrations

Maps
Cornwall and the Isles of Scilly, showing the principal ports 10 & 11
Isles of Scilly, showing main islands only 44
Map of sea journey to the Scilly Isles (by courtesy of I.S.S. Co. Ltd.) 45
Inshore dinghy marks on the Isles of Scilly 47
Deep sea angling marks on the Isles of Scilly 55

Photographs (see between pages 40 & 41)

A fine ling taken out of Penzance (by courtesy of Albert Southwell) 14
A happy group of Mount's Bay Anglers (by courtesy of Roy Powell)
Hayle anglers returning to Falmouth (by courtesy of Albert Southwell)
Tony Blewett playing a coalfish (by courtesy of Tony Blewett)
'The Talisman' entering Mousehole (by courtesy of Phil Wallis)
Pollack and ling from Mount's Bay (by courtesy of Roy Powell)
Nicky Morse with two fine coalfish (by courtesy of Nicky Morse)
A 35½lb conger from inshore wreck (by courtesy of Roy Powell)
Luke Piantino with an inshore plaice (by courtesy of Mark Piantino)
'The happy dinghy anglers' (Mount's Bay) (by courtesy of M. Sorrentino)
Plaice and turbot taken off Aire Point (by courtesy of A. Piantino)
Mark Piantino with two nice pouting (by courtesy of Luke Piantino)
'Dab Hands', fishing in Mount's Bay (by courtesy of Mark Piantino)
Tony Blewett with record coalfish (by courtesy of Tony Blewett)
Sid Pender with record scad (by courtesy of Luke Piantino)
Two small inshore ray from Sennen Cove (by courtesy of A. Piantino)
Mr. L. Nardini with National Record garfish (by courtesy of Peter Maddern)
Sid Pender receiving J. Eathorne Trophy (by courtesy of David Cains)
Tony Blewett with National Record Opah (by courtesy of Tony Blewett)
Clive James with local record cod (by courtesy of Clive James)
Sid Pender receiving the Clifford Cory Cup (by courtesy of David Cains)
View of Penzance Heliport (by courtesy of British Airways)
Dinghy fishing in Scillonian waters (by courtesy of Ken Allison)
'Conger by night' (by courtesy of John Poynter)
A brace of good ling (by courtesy of John Poynter)
A fine Scillonian garfish (by courtesy of John Poynter)
Two good pollack from Scillonian waters (by courtesy of John Poynter)
A fine 'blue' from Scillonian waters (by courtesy of John Poynter)

7

Acknowledgements

The author wishes to acknowledge the help and advice given by the following persons in the compilation of the text and the provision of many of the photographs:

Eddy Anstey, Resorts Officer, Penwith District Council
The staff of British Airways, The Heliport, Eastern Green, Penzance
Frank Gibson for photographs and professional advice
Ivan Glover, Chief Executive, Isles of Scilly Council
Sandy Leventon, Editor of *Sea Angling Monthly*, for permission to reproduce sections which had previously been published as articles in that magazine
The following fellow-members of the Mount's Bay Angling Society: Tony Blewett, David Cains, Clive James, George and Peter Maddern, Nicky Morse, Mark and Luke Piantino, Roy Powell; also Frank and Phil Wallis of Mousehole and fellow-angler Ken Allison
Jeff Nicholls, Manager, Isles of Scilly Steamship Company Office, Penzance
The late John Ozard, founder member of the Isles of Scilly Angling Club
Melvyn Russ, Features Editor of the *Angler's Mail*, for permission to reproduce sections which had previously been published as articles in that magazine
The following Scillonians, past and present: Paddy Daly, Eric Guy, Lou Hichens, Joe Hicks, Lloyd Hicks, Mike Hicks, Richard Lethbridge, Reggie Phillips, John Poynter, Ronald Simons, Mr Sissam, Verney Thompson, Jimmy Williams
Albert Southwell, Hon. Sec., Hayle Sea Angling Club

Introduction

THE SOUTH WEST is the most popular region in the whole of the British Isles for tourists from home and abroad. From the sea angler's point of view it is also the most lucrative and prolific region for specimen fish and record catches. Add these two aspects together and you have in Cornwall and the Isles of Scilly not only an area of outstanding beauty which appeals to the general holiday maker, but a 'country apart' which offers the visiting angler (and his family) the best of both worlds.

Angling is the greatest participant sport in the country with some three million club members and possibly as many, if not more, non-club members. The number of sea anglers actively engaged in the sport has increased rapidly over the past ten years as charter boat facilities have improved and more facilities have been made available for the visiting small-boat angler to launch his own craft.

As a result of this increased participation the number of different species being brought to the scales has also increased in proportion. Indeed the County Record Lists show that 65 different species of fish have been recorded from both boat and shore, probably the highest number of different species for any coastal region of the British Isles. The number of record fish being accepted nationally is growing each year and a high percentage of these record fish are taken from the coastal waters here in the far south-west. Species, which until a few years ago were considered rarities, are now appearing more regularly as more and more sea anglers go further in search of their sport. Over the past five years such semi-tropical species as the bogue, trigger fish, opah and wreckfish have been taken from Cornish waters.

The National Rod-Caught Record List shows that one third of the record fish taken on rod and line in the British Isles were taken from south-western waters, with Cornwall and Devon sharing the honours equally. This total of 50 record fish is unequalled in any other region of the British Isles.

Although there are no record fish listed as having been caught from the waters around the Isles of Scilly potential record fish have been landed but unfortunately the correct procedure for weighing the fish and having them ratified was not followed. The position of the islands, at the junction of the English and Bristol Channels, implies that the migratory species coming into British waters during the spring and summer months would pass either to the north or the south of the islands. It is therefore logical to assume that the Scilly Isles are ideally situated for the dedicated sea angler who might set out to hunt for specimen fish and possibly break an existing British record.

> The message to the sea angler is obvious, your chances of catching a specimen or record fish are much better in the waters off Cornwall and the Isles of Scilly than anywhere else in the British Isles

Cornwall and the Isles of Scilly showing the main ports

1 Deep Sea Fishing from Cornish Ports

THE LONG, indented Cornish coastline jutting out into the warming influence of the Gulf Stream offers the visiting angler the choice of many ports from which charter boats operate. Here in the far south-west the sea angler has a wider choice of species than anywhere else in the British Isles.

There are three main branches of the sport of sea angling available to the visiting deep sea angler, i.e. wreck-fishing, reef-fishing and sharking. Most of the major Cornish ports on both the south and north coast offer some or all of these facilities.

Each District Council in Cornwall is responsible for the annual relicensing of the boatmen and charter skippers who operate in its administrative area. These licences are revised and reviewed regularly so that the visiting angler is advised to check locally before going to sea. Current details will be found in the section entitled 'Useful Addresses'.

Although the Cornish port of Looe is synonymous with shark fishing in the minds of most sea anglers, the charter fleet skippers offer a choice of fishing. Boats operating from the port often join the Plymouth-based fleet in fishing the prolific grounds around the Eddystone and other mid-Channel areas which produce good catches of wreck fish such as pollack, ling and in season, of course, near-record coalfish. Charter boats based in Mevagissey and Fowey have also built up a nationally respected reputation for consistently good wreck catches over the past ten years or so. Although some angling writers believe that the hey-day of wreck-fishing has passed, due to over-fishing by sea anglers and commercial fishermen, especially with the introduction of wreck-nets and, to a greater extent, gill-nets, there are still virgin wrecks available for the dedicated charter skipper to explore. Although it means more steaming from port to fishing grounds many charter skippers have kept abreast of the times and have invested heavily in modern, faster custom-built angling boats to get their customers to and from the grounds in half the time so allowing more time for fishing. It also means that when the weather is changeable, especially during the winter months when specimen pollack and coalfish are at their peak, the anglers can often reach the marks and return in safety before the weather worsens, which would have been impossible (say) ten years ago with the more traditional craft. Some of the charter skippers working from Plymouth and south Cornish ports now also offer extended trips to mid-Channel wrecks, the Channel Islands and even week-long charter trips to the Isles of Scilly.

Charter trips are also available from the picturesque village of Polperro. Full details are available either from the appropriate District Council or from the harbourside at Looe, Fowey, Mevagissey and Polperro.

Falmouth Harbour is one of the best natural harbours in the world. In its time it has been a clipper port of some renown, a tanker repair base and in more recent times its possibilities as an oil-drilling base have been considered. During the past few years, with the development of the winter mackerel fishery, the port has played host to many Eastern Bloc and foreign factory ships. Commercial fishing in the port has received a boost and there has also been a spin-off in the direction of charter boat fishing.

There is a thriving Boatmen's Association in Falmouth and full details are available around the entrance to the Prince of Wales Pier. Many good fish have been taken by boat anglers from the general area of Falmouth Bay where there are one or two inshore wrecks, relics of the heavy air-raids which the area experienced during the Second World War.

Between The Lizard and Falmouth lie the group of rocks known as 'The Manacles'. These rocks are infamous for the number of wrecks which occurred there during the days of sail, when many hundreds of lives were lost. The general area, however, offers excellent fishing under the guidance of experienced local boatmen operating either out of Falmouth or from the small fishing village of Coverack. 'The Manacles' have produced large bass and pollack on the drift as well as other species such as red and black bream. There are also excellent turbot grounds off-shore within the range of private craft as well as charter boats. Specimen whiting, hake and haddock have also been recorded from anglers working out of Falmouth. Three years ago Porthleven anglers also 'struck gold' with their haddock catches, landing eight gold medals, three silver medals and a bronze for the specie with fish ranging in weight from 6–10–8 to 13–2–4. Catches the following year ranged from 7–5–0 to 12–12–0. The best rod-caught turbot recorded from Cornish waters weighed 28–8–0 and the national boat-caught record whiting of 6–12–0 was landed by an angler fishing out of Falmouth.

The eastern side of Mount's Bay, off Porthleven, produces good catches of spurdog at peak periods of the year. Last winter saw exceptional landings by the local commercial fleet with a total of 25,000 stone being landed in a two-day period. This winter a single day's landing totalled 13,000 stone. The county record for the specie taken from a boat stands at 21–3–8.

In Penwith waters the areas around the Longships and Wolf Rock Lighthouses off Land's End produce good pollack and coalfish, usually taken on redgills on the drift. The area just to the east of Land's End marked with the Runnelstone Buoy is a noted hot-spot for bass and red bream and is extensively fished by the commercial fishermen from Penberth Cove. Because of the strong tidal flow in the area and its exposed position this area is best fished with a professional skipper. Several of the Penzance-based charter boats offer shark fishing as well as wrecking and reef-fishing. Wreck-fishing trips in the area have produced specimen coalfish, pollack, conger, ling and cod. Former Mount's Bay Angling Society chairman, Tony Blewett, holder of the national record for the opah, with a fish of 128–0–0, also caught the best coalfish from Penwith waters which weighed 25–13–0. MBAS club member Malcolm Jones, a keen boat angler, last year broke the local club record for the pollack with a fine specimen of 19–9–6. Other local club records stand at conger (50–0–0); ling (37–0–0) and cod 36–4–0. County records for these species are:- coalfish 28–11–12; pollack 24–8–0; conger 84–4–0; ling 43–2–0 and cod 36–4–0. The county boat record for the bass is 12–10–12 while the record for the black bream stands at 5–4–8 and the record for the red bream is exactly six pounds.

During 1981 the following fish were registered by anglers of Cornish clubs affiliated to the Cornish Division of the National Federation of Sea Anglers.

Greater weaver 1–6–12; Whiting 6–12–0; Red Bream 4–8–0; Thornback ray 15–10–0; Scad 2–2–0; Turbot 20–4–0; Brill 5–5–0; Hake 10–8–0; Pollack 19–8–8; Coalfish 22–8–0; Ling 37–14–0 and Pouting 3–6–12.

C. Allen of the Hayle Sea Angling Club with a fine ling of 30-9-0 caught out of Penzance aboard the M.V. Hustler. Photograph taken outside the 'Quay Shop', a fishing tackle shop run by Johnny Wing in Quay Street, Penzance.

All these fish were landed by members of affiliated clubs in the western half of the Duchy but possibly as many, if not better fish were landed by boat anglers representing clubs east of Truro. Details of catches from charter-boats working out of Mevagissey, Looe, Fowey and Polperro are often included in the angling news and reviews of the Plymouth area.

Good catches of ray and turbot are also made by local commercial boats fishing grounds off the Longships Lighthouse and further up the coast from Land's End to Pendeen Watch. Charter boats from Penzance often work the areas around the Longships and the Wolf. In fine weather these areas are also in the range of the smaller boats kept in the many coves around the coast.

Charter and self-hire facilities are available at the very popular sea-side resort of St. Ives. As the economic importance of the town as a fishing port has declined, the popularity of the town as a holiday centre has grown. Although the local fishing fleet is numerically smaller than in the hey-day of the pilchard and herring fleets, the local boats bring home good catches of prime fish. Good ray and turbot fishing is available through the local charterboat skippers as well as mixed ground bottom fishing. During last year's M.B.A.S. Annual Angling Festival one local angler weighed in a brace of good fish, a bass from his own boat of just under nine pounds plus a double figure turbot. One popular area in St. Ives Bay is that around 'The Stones', a group of rocks and ledges in the middle of the outer reaches of St. Ives Bay. Most of the bay, however, offers clean sand bottom for ray and various species of flats.

The other two major north Cornish ports offering charter facilities are Newquay and Padstow. Newquay formerly produced the old British Records for the pollack and coalfish before wreck fishing became popular. The current boat record lesser spotted-dogfish of 4–1–0 was taken out of Newquay by B. Solomon.

While Looe is synonymous with fishing for blue sharks Padstow can rightly be known as the 'Mecca' for those anglers wishing to do battle with porbeagles. Padstow holds the port record for the porbeagle with a fish of 465 lbs as well as the record for the best one-day aggregate by one angler set in 1981.

The following British Record fish have been taken by anglers operating from the main ports in Cornwall.

Opah	128–0–0	Tony Blewett	Mount's Bay
Electric Ray	96–1–0	N. Cowley	Mevagissey
Blue shark	218–0–0	N. Sutcliffe	Looe
Spurdog	21–3–8	P. Barrett	Porthleven
Whiting	6–12–0	N. Croft	Falmouth
Flounder	5–11–0	A. Cobbledick	Fowey
G. Forkbeard	4–11–0	M. Woodgate	Falmouth
Haddock	13–11–0	B. Bones	Falmouth
Ling	57–2–0	H. Solomons	Mevagissey
Anglerfish	82–12–0	K. Ponsford	Mevagissey
Gilthead Bream	5–0–0	A. Stratton-Knott	St. Mawes
Comber	1–13–0	B. Phillips	Mount's Bay
Red Bream	9–8–0	B. Reynolds	Mevagissey
Bull-Huss	21–3–0	J. Holmes	Looe
Garfish	3–2–0	L. Nardini	Mount's Bay
Porbeagle	465–0–0	J. Potier	Padstow

2 Shark Fishing in Cornish Waters

ALTHOUGH LOOE is recognised as the centre for shark fishing in the minds of most anglers there are other Cornish ports which offer similar facilities. Padstow as a centre for fishing for porbeagles has already been mentioned.

Looe achieved national and international fame because its charter skippers were the first to realise the potential of what was then a new form of angling. Although Looe is still considered to be the headquarters of sharking in the British Isles other Cornish ports also have reputations of which they can be justly proud. Padstow has justly gained the reputation of being the premier port in the country for its catches of porbeagles while Looe still holds the national record for the 'blue'.

Other north coast ports which offer sharking trips are Newquay and St. Ives. As most porbeagle catches are made off the north Cornish coast it is fair to assume that anglers working from these two ports would also stand a reasonable chance of contacting these fish.

Besides Looe, the following south coast ports offer sharking facilities on modern, well-equipped craft – Mevagissey, Polperro, Falmouth, Penzance and Mousehole.

Phil and Frank Wallis have been running charter trips from Mousehole for over twenty years. They offer wrecking, reefing and general bottom-fishing as well as sharking. Last year their best two specimen blue sharks weighed 178 lbs and 135 lbs and were both taken on the same day. Their largest ever blue shark weighed in at 196 lbs. The best porbeagle weighed 170 lbs and their most unusual catch was a 9–8–0 stone bass or wreckfish. The Wallis Bros. are members of the Shark Club of Great Britain and commence their sharking season on June 1st. Providing the summer is warm their season will last until the early part of October. July is considered to be the best month for specimen sharks with the late summer and autumn producing more fish but of smaller size. Their best daily 'bag' consisted of 45 blue shark taken by three rods in just three hours fishing time. They offer shark fishing trips to school parties at reduced rates. They can be contacted on Penzance 731511.

From Penzance there are several charter boats offering sharking trips. The Mishana, Mermaid, Hustler, Silver Spray and several others are all modern, fully equipped vessels complying with Board of Trade regulations. Skipper/owner Chris Thomas was Cornish Boat Angling Champion for three consecutive years during the late 1970s.

As the summer approaches sharks move into the waters around our coasts from the deeper water of the South Western Approaches chasing the shoals of mackerel, pilchards and, to a lesser extent, herring on which they feed. It is therefore logical to suggest that the further south and west you travel the greater the chance of making contact with these fish. Therefore, because of its geographical location, Cornwall, with its long coastline and many sheltered harbours and coves, is the ideal base from which to set out on shark fishing expeditions.

Although Looe has an established sharking record it is an often over-looked fact that the ports of Penzance and Mousehole, situated in Mount's Bay, are nearly sixty miles further to the south and west and therefore nearer the fishing areas. This is an important point for any prospective shark angler to bear in mind, especially during the earlier part of the season, i.e. June and July when the larger fish are likely to be taken.

Shark fishing from the Isles of Scilly has not been exploited in the same way as it has been on the mainland, however, I am sure that it must hold tremendous potential. What little shark fishing has been tried has produced good results. Because Scilly virtually bisects the flow of the Gulf Stream as it passes to the north into the Bristol Channel and to the south up the English Channel, it is safe to assume that the porbeagles, blues and makos taken in Cornish waters must have passed through Scillonian waters earlier in the season.

Some mainland sharking skippers have to steam up to twelve miles from their home port before reaching the areas where the sharks are feeding. On Scilly the same areas, usually those with an average depth of over forty fathoms, are found within four miles of the south coast of the islands.

3 Inshore Fishing in Cornish Waters

THERE HAS been an increase in the popularity of all forms of water sports during the past ten years or so. This is reflected in the growing number of small-boat owners who now trail their craft with them on holiday to sample what is on offer in parts of the country other than their own immediate district. Many local sailing clubs have regular seasonal visitors and the number of visiting small-boat anglers is also on the increase.

Many of the larger Cornish ports have launching facilities for small-boat owners and visiting dinghy anglers can use these facilities at an agreed daily or weekly rate. In some areas there are also secure 'holding-pens' for dinghies when not in use. There is only a small number of moorings available in some harbours for visiting small boats.

Any visiting angler contemplating bringing his own boat to Cornwall to fish the estuaries and sheltered inshore waters around the coast should first check with the appropriate local authority as to the facilities available before setting out. In the larger harbours permission should always be sought from the Harbour Master. Details giving rates of daily charges, local byelaws etc are usually displayed either in or near the Harbour Office. In some of the smaller, more remote coves the permission of the local farmer or land owner should be sought. Quite often launching a dinghy presents little or no difficulty, it's getting the boat back to the car that can present problems!! Obviously the visiting angler should check on the possible use of a winch or tractor before setting off and should also check the tides so that he is not stranded on soft bottom well away from the standing 'hard' or the slipway.

Fishing from a small boat in unfamiliar waters can present problems, even to the experienced dinghy angler, and local advice should always be sought before setting out. Local weather forecasts can be obtained from the local 'met' office or from the Coastguard. If there is any doubt at all about the weather – leave it for another day.

The coastal waters of Cornwall offer the visiting dinghy angler more species than perhaps any other inshore section of the British coast line. In the course of a season the dedicated dinghy angler may take up to thirty different species.

Although the waters off the south coast are more sheltered than those off the rather exposed north coast, the north coast often gives better quality fish during fine weather. With the prevailing wind usually between north-west and south-west any stretch of Cornish coast facing between north-east and south-east would offer sheltered water sufficiently far enough offshore to suit the small-boat angler.

Inshore fishing is likely to produce some of the following species:- anglerfish, bass, bogue, red and black bream, bull huss, coalfish, dab, flounder, conger, garfish, red and grey gurnards, ling, mackerel, red and grey mullet, plaice, pollack, pouting, scad, spurdog, whiting, cuckoo, ballan and corkwing wrasse, lesser-spotted-dogfish, rockling, weaver, tub gurnard, small-eyed ray, cuckoo ray, thornback ray and blonde ray.

Fishing over soft ground with worm baits would account for dabs, flounder, red and grey gurnard, plaice, lesser-spotted-dogfish and whiting. Fish bait on the same ground takes the same species with perhaps the exception of flounders and plaice which seem to have a strong preference for worm baits in our waters.

Fishing hard ground would produce red and black bream, bull huss, coalfish, ling, conger, pollack, pouting, rockling and various species of wrasse. Fish baits are recommended for bream, bull huss, conger and ling while the other species can be taken on worms.

Spinning with fish strip, king-rag or artificial lures takes pollack, coalfish, scad, mackerel and garfish.

Off the north coast many venues offer turbot and ray fishing close to the shore. This coast is exposed and should be fished after you have gained local knowledge of the likely conditions. Sandy areas will provide dabs, plaice, turbot, brill and various species of ray. Dogfish will be taken and there is always the possibility of a tope – although they are not fished for deliberately. During exceptionally hot summers other, less common species, such as the bogue, triggerfish, comber, wreckfish and opah have been taken in Cornish waters.

There is enough variety to cater for the needs of most visiting dinghy anglers who will find local fishermen, boatmen and club anglers only too willing to pass on advice.

Estuary Fishing

The estuaries of the major Cornish rivers offer the visiting small-boat angler the chance to fish in sheltered conditions when fishing in the open sea may be impossible. Obviously the visitor should check his tides and the rate of tidal flow before setting out and ascertain whether there are any dangers such as sandbanks, tide-rips or 'bars' at the seaward end of the river of which he should be made aware.

Most of the estuaries hold flounders and mullet, with the deep-water marks producing plaice, bull-huss, dogfish, ray and conger. Specimen flounders are taken from both banks of the River Tamar during the autumn and winter. Thornbacks are taken in spring and early summer being followed by bass. Conger are taken throughout the year, especially if the weather is mild.

The ancient town of Fowey, with its deep water estuary, offers excellent fishing to the dinghy angler. On the eastern side of the river lies the village of Polruan. The bottom reaches of the river offer fishing when the conditions on the open coast are unfavourable. Upstream at Golant there are extensive sandbanks where specimen flounders are regularly taken. The long-standing National Boat Record fish was taken here. Further downstream, between Golant and the Old Sawmills, plaice and flounders are often caught. Large conger are also taken from the river in the general area of the E.C.L.P. loading jetties. Although ragworm is a favoured bait for flounders in many parts of the county those at Golant have been taken on sandeels.

St. Mawes lies on the eastern side of the deep water estuary of the River Fal. It is a popular sailing and boating area and visiting dinghy anglers would find launching facilities here. The area of Trefusis Point, inside the estuary on the Flushing shore, offers good sport for pollack, wrasse, bass and flounders. The Penryn Channel also produces good flounders while the deep water marks in other parts of the estuary hold thornback ray and large conger. Further upstream towards Truro and Malpas there are other marks which produce flounders and mullet. A baited spoon worked over the bottom should take flounders with ragworm being the recommended bait here.

The Helford River and neighbouring Gillan Creek are best fished for mullet and flounders over the top of the tide in the upper reaches although the lower reaches can be fished on the early flood. The lower reaches of the Helford River have produced bass and thornback ray. Fishing the entrances to the creeks offers the chance of taking pollack, mackerel, bass and wrasse with the possibility of conger on fish baits after dark. St. Antony Narrows offers good fishing on the flood tide for bass, flounders and mullet although bottom fishing is difficult due to the presence of bait-robbing crabs. Self-hire boats are available from the Jenkin family at S. Antony.

The north coast estuaries of the River Hayle and the River Gannel, near Newquay, are too shallow and heavily silted to offer safe dinghy fishing. The River Camel which flows through Camelford and Wadebridge before entering the sea below Padstow can be fished in the lower reaches using Padstow Harbour as a base. The area produces bass, flounders and grey mullet. The tidal flow is particularly strong, especially with the ebb tide in conjunction with the flow of the river.

Visiting dinghy anglers intending to fish any of the Cornish estuaries should obtain local advice from the appropriate Harbour Office.

Inshore Dinghy Fishing in Penwith Waters

Fourteen years ago I was fortunate enough to be able to return to work and live in my own part of Cornwall. During this period, after four years on the Isles of Scilly, I have been able to fish the inshore waters of West Penwith from my own dinghies. I have one dinghy based at Mousehole on the shores of Mount's Bay while the second one is based at Sennen Cove, just north of Land's End. Thus I have the best of both worlds, being able to fish which ever side of the Land's End Peninsula is sheltered from the prevailing winds. The species available on either side of the peninsula vary so that one has a wider choice of fish.

Although the sheltered waters of Mount's Bay can be fished more often than the exposed waters off the north coast, the north coast does offer better quality fish during fine weather periods.

Mount's Bay is the first bay along the south coast when approached from the west. It sweeps in an arc from Land's End in the west round to the Lizard in the south east. Although the outer areas of the bay are exposed to the prevailing winds, mainly from the south west, the inner part of the bay, within a line from Lamorna Cove in the west to Cudden Point in the east offers dinghy fishing in comparatively sheltered waters for the visiting angler. The western side of Mount's Bay, from Lamorna Cove into Penzance, is sheltered with the wind between south-west and north-west and during the summer months this area is fishable for weeks on end.

Although many visiting anglers rely on the charter skippers for their sport, and fishing holiday-makers try feathering for mackerel from pleasure boats, there is a growing number of dinghy small-boat owners who take their craft in tow to explore sea areas other than their own familiar waters. Mount's Bay offers these anglers good fishing together with facilities for digging bait and for launching dinghies. There are slipways for launching small craft in Penzance, Newlyn and Mousehole harbours and at Lamorna Cove and Sennen Cove. There is usually a daily charge for visitors and of course the harbour authorities should be consulted prior to use of the slip. Small craft may also be launched from the Eastern Green Beach between Penzance and Marazion. This area comes under the juridiction of Penwith District Council whose offices are at St. Clare, Penzance.

There is at present no bait shortage in this part of Cornwall. Natural baits are available in the district and include fresh mackerel, sandeels, whiteworm, ragworm, lugworm and peeler and soft-back crabs. White rag may be dug between Marazion and St. Michael's Mount harbour while the whole of the Eastern Green Beach provides lugworm. Lugworm and ragworm may be dug in the principal harbours of Penzance, Newlyn and Mousehole although there are local restrictions posted at each harbour side. Fresh supplies of mackerel are usually available either from the quayside, the market area at Newlyn or from the local fishmongers' shops. Fresh or frozen sandeels may be purchased from local tackle shops or obtained from the beaches between Hayle and St. Ives or at Sennen Cove. These venues are all on the north coast.

In Mount's Bay the spring tides average 18 feet, rising to a maximum of 20 feet during the autumn. Neap tides vary from 12 feet to 14 feet throughout the year. Spring tides naturally offer more scope for bait collecting and are generally conducive to spinning while neap tides make worm digging difficult but are ideal for bottom fishing.

The tidal streams along the coast from Lamorna to Penzance run in a SW/NE direction. The tide does not make at a uniform speed. Taking an 18 foot spring tide as an example the following tide flow figures would apply. 1st hour 1/12th – 1ft 6in; 2nd hour 2/12ths – 3 feet; 3rd hour 3/12ths – 4ft 6in; 4th hour 3/12ths – 4ft 6in; 5th hour 2/12ths – 3 feet and 6th hour 1/12th – 1ft 6in. It will be noticed therefore that half of the flood tide makes during the third and fourth hours which would be the best time to fish on the drift when spinning. The corresponding hours also apply to the ebb.

Along the western shore of Mount's Bay the flood tide makes along the shore while the last of the ebb is running out approximately 400 metres off shore. If this early flood is fished on the drift with a south-westerly wind one can spin for mackerel and garfish on practically one continuous drift from Lamorna Cove to St. Michael's Mount. Garfish are usually taken on ragworm or thin mackerel strip in the top two fathoms of water while the mackerel are taken at varying depths. In 1980 a garfish exceeding four pounds in weight was taken on commercial feathers just off Mousehole (St. Clement's) Island while in 1981 a rod caught specimen was landed by a visitor weighing over three pounds.

It is better to bottom fish over either the high water or low water slack period on a neap tide. High water springs usually occur when high tide is between 5–7 pm with the corresponding low water at lunch time. Neap tides will produce high water over the midday period. There is approximately 6½ hours between high and low water.

Charts of Mount's Bay may be purchased from local booksellers and chandlers. The Admiralty Chart No. 2345, with topography taken from the local Ordnance Survey map of the area shows the waters of Mount's Bay (Penzance Bay) from Tater Dhu lighthouse, just west of Lamorna Cove, to the back of St. Michael's Mount. The corresponding adjacent sheet would give details of the eastern part of the bay. However, for the visiting dinghy angler based in Penzance, Newlyn, Mousehole or Marazion the former chart is sufficient. The tide table is reproduced in the local weekly paper.

Within a line drawn from the end of Newlyn Lighthouse Pier (South) to

St. Michael's Mount the depth is less than six fathoms. Inside this line there are rocky ledges which mostly show at low water spring tides. From Newlyn, working east they are Lariggan Rocks; Dog Rock; Gear Rocks; Cressar Rocks; Raymond Rocks; Long Rock; Outer Penzeath Rock; Hogus Rocks and the ledges behind and to the east of St. Michael's Mount. Between Marazion and Cudden Point there are several more rocks and ledges, the principal one being the Crebe off Perranuthnoe. Around and outside these ledges the bottom is mainly a mixture of sand and shingle.

Along the western shore from Newlyn to Lamorna Cove the six fathom line skirts the shore, goes around the back of Mousehole (St. Clement's) Island and then runs in to within one hundred metres of the cliffs. Between Newlyn and Mousehole there are two ledges of note. Carn Base and the Lowlee Ledges lie in a line approximately due SE from Newlyn Lighthouse Pier. Carn Base is off Penlee Quarry while the Lowlee Ledges lie inside the buoy marking their position. There is shallow water between Mousehole and its island. Between Mousehole and Lamorna there are three drying ledges to be avoided. Off Penzer Point, below the Coastguard Lookout, there are Penzer Ledges which dry after half tide. Between 'the trees' and Carn Dhu lies Kemyll Rock, or The Kellin, which only breaks on a low water spring tide. Just off Carn Dhu, to the west there is The Heaver which dries three feet. Off Tater Dhu Lighthouse lie the two Bucks Rocks. On the eastern side of the bay there is very shoal water between Cudden Point and Porthleven, the main ledges being marked by the 'Mountamopus' buoy. Outside a line drawn from the Lowlee buoy to the back of Mousehole Island the bottom shelves away from ten to twenty fathoms. The bottom is mainly of mud with odd patches of gravel and shingle. There are also one or two patches of rough ground due SE of Mousehole Island. A group of four 'pinnacles' lies about a quarter of a mile NE of the Lowlee.

The 'hard' ground marks of Carn Base, Lowlee and its neighbouring ledges, plus the rough ground areas towards the middle of the bay will produce pollack, various types of wrasse, pouting, conger, bream and the occasional ling. The larger areas of soft bottom provide good catches of plaice, dabs, various types of gurnard and of course lesser spotted dogfish. Occasional tope are also taken and the eastern waters of the bay off Porthleven are noted for their catches of specimen spur dogs. Some ray and turbot are taken on sand patches behind the ledges off St. Michael's Mount. Flounders and plaice are likely to be caught along the whole length of the Eastern Green which runs from Penzance to Marazion. This area also produces pollack and bass when trolling, especially off the rocky ledges previously mentioned. Black conger are also taken on the rough ground along the western shore. Carn Petrel, which lies just offshore of Kemyll Rock is a handy rough ground mark for the dinghy angler as it can be fished with the wind between SW and NW in reasonable comfort when it would be too risky to venture further out into the bay.

Between Penlee Point and the Lowlee Ledges lies an area of sand known locally as 'No Rest' as it was continually trawled years ago when the small inshore trawlers could not fish outside marks because of bad weather. Over the past three years I have taken a total of 120 plaice and 330 dabs from this area together with the soft ground marks behind Mousehole Island. The best dabs weighed in at 1-7-0 and 1-6-4 with the best rod caught plaice scaling 4-8-0 and 4-6-0. My biggest plaice ever taken from No Rest was on a set ground line and weighed 6-2-0. Between Mousehole and its island there is a small patch of sand known locally as 'The Drethen'. It can easily be found at lowish tide. It offers mackerel, garfish and pollack on spinning tackle with plaice, flounders and occasional sole being taken on the bottom. The weedy fringes also produce good wrasse. It has also produced the odd stray Anglerfish to 18-8-0. One favourite hot-spot for big wrasse used to be the area just off the northern end of the island where the lobster fishermen keep their store-pots. Wrasse to 6-2-0 have been taken here on rod.

Another rough ground mark known as 'The Stennack' lies between Lamorna Cove and Tater Dhu. It is marked on the chart and offers sheltered fishing with the wind from the North West. It is often trolled for pollack by commercial fishermen using redgills or red rubber baits. Spinning over rough ground in shallow waters using ragworm, king ragworm or small strips of mackerel will take pollack, mackerel, garfish and scad especially if the light is fading from the sky. Spinning over soft ground during the middle of the day is likely to produce mackerel and garfish only. Bottom fishing over rough or hard ground with lugworm bait will produce various types of wrasse, pouting, poor cod (or Bib) while a change to mackerel strip would encourage cuckoo wrasse, conger and ling to come on the feed. Although I prefer to fish for flats from an anchored dinghy it is possible to bottom fish on the drIft providing the tidal movement and wind drift are suitable. Soft bottom ledgering with worm baits will produce plaice, dabs, whiting etc while fish baits encourage further dabs, whiting, gurnards, lesser spotted dogfish, grey gurnards, streaked gurnards and red gurnards. Tub gurnards are also sometimes taken. During the late sixties it was commonplace to catch 'stones' of red bream from the inshore marks of Mount's Bay. Unfortunately the fish now seem to have moved out into deeper water and are now only taken on deep water reef marks. The occasional bream can be taken, however, on the rough ground marks due SE of Mousehole Island. One good mark is to line up St.Mary's Church, Penzance with the Lowlee Buoy and steam SE from the island until the large guest house is directly over the cave at Mousehole. As a check one can then see along the coast beyond Tater Dhu lighthouse in the west as far as the Logan Rock at Porthcurno. To line up

Carn Petrel off Lamorna one should get the white house on the western side of Lamorna Cove in the 'saddle' of Carn Dhu, with the large grey guest house on the front at Mousehole just showing clear of Penzer Point.

During the past few years the following species have been taken on rod and line in the inner areas of Mount's Bay.

Angler Fish (18-8-0); Bass (8-0-0); Black Bream (3-10-0); Red Bream (1-8-0); Bull Huss (15-0-0); Coalfish (up to 3-8-0); Cod (4-0-0); Conger (35-8-0); Dab (1-8-0); L.S.D. (2-11-0); Flounder (2-3-1); Garfish (up to 3-3-0); Grey Gurnard (1-2-3); Red Gurnard (2-0-0); Streaked Gurnard (0-10-8); Tub Gurnard (1-9-8); Ling (12-0-0); Mackerel (up to 2-12-0); Red Mullet (1-0-0); Plaice (4-8-0); Pollack (up to 4-8-0); Pouting (2-8-0); Thornback Ray (up to 12-0-0); Three Bearded Rockling (1-6-8); Scad (up to 1-8-0); Spurdog (up to 14-0-0); Whiting (up to 3-8-0); Ballan Wrasse (6-2-0); Cuckoo Wrasse (1-8-0); Corkwing Wrasse (0-8-0); Common Sole (2-15-12).

Other species caught include Gilthead Bream; Comber; Silver Eel; Lesser Forkbeard; Greater Weaver; Haddock; Herring; Lumpsucker; Golden Grey Mullet; Grey Mullet; Pilchard; Blonde Ray; Spotted Ray; Cuckoo Ray; Thornback Ray; Twaite and Allis Shad; Smoothhound; Sole; Sunfish; Tope; File or Trigger Fish; Turbot; and a Wreck Fish.

Personal bests for the species mentioned include the following specimens i.e. dab (1-7-0); flounder (2-3-1); grey gurnard (1-2-3); streaked gurnard (0-12-0); plaice (4-8-0) and ballan wrasse (6-2-0). At 31st December 1981 I held the County Boat Records for the bogue, herring, three-bearded rockling; corkwing wrasse; triggerfish; streaked gurnard; grey gurnard and the scad. All these fish were taken dinghy fishing on light tackle in the inshore water around the Land's End district.

Local club records for inshore species include bogue (1-6-3); bull huss (17-4-0); comber (1-0-8); dab (1-7-0); silver eel (1-7-0); flounder (2-15-12); garfish (1-13-8); grey gurnard (1-2-3); red gurnard (2-13-0); Lesser spotted dog (2-11-0); mackerel (2-11-15); grey mullet (3-14-12); plaice (4-8-0); pouting (3-10-4); rockling (1-6-14); scad (1-15-2); twaite shad (1-4-0); allis shad (1-4-0); spurdog (13-6-0); sole (2-15-12); triggerfish (2-6-7); weaver (1-15-4); whiting (4-0-0); ballan wrasse (6-9-9); cuckoo wrasse (1-15-0); and streaked gurnard (0-12-0).

Inshore Dinghy Fishing from Sennen Cove

Sennen Cove is a picturesque fishing village situated about one mile north of Land's End. Although its importance as a commercial fishing village has declined over the years it has become one of the most popular holiday spots in the whole of West Cornwall. The small harbour is protected by a breakwater which offers some shelter to the small fleet of commercial boats still working from this remote corner of the Cornish coast. Besides the commercial boats there are about two dozen other small boats which are used either on a part-time or pleasure basis. From the cove the gentle sweep of Whitesand Bay leads around to Aire Point in the north, approximately one third of the way towards Cape Cornwall, the next major headland. Off the only Cape in southern Britain lie The Brisons, two foreboding rocks which mark the northern extremity of the bay.

Sennen Village lies at the top of the steep, one-in-six hill leading down to the Cove. Visiting anglers should turn right down the Cove Road opposite the local primary school at the top of the hill. Access from Penzance simply means following the main A30 road as far as the school. There are two large car-parks in Sennen Cove, one at the bottom of the hill and the other at the far end of the Cove. During the high season these parks are usually full before 10.30am. There is an overspill car-park at the top of the hill on the right hand side.

There are two slipways in the Cove. The major part of the slip is used for launching the local boats. However, there is a smaller, steeper slipway next to the breakwater which may be used by visiting small boat owners. A notice board in the Cove states the conditions laid down by the Harbour Commissioners for use of the facilities by visitors. Prior permission to launch a boat should first be obtained from the harbour master, Mr James Nicholas, who lives in Bay View, Sennen Cove. Sennen Cove waters are open to the full fury of the Atlantic Ocean and heavy swells break on off-shore reefs. Local advice should always be sought even during the fine summer period before setting afloat. It is best fished with an off-shore wind between north-east and south-east with no ground swell.

Baits available locally include sandeels, taken from the nearby beach as well as small quantities of ragworm and lugworm which can be found under the rocks in and around the harbour. Small mackerel can often be purchased from the local fishermen who usually land their fish during the summer at approximately mid-morning. Soft-backed and peeler crabs may also be found under stones along the rocky foreshore. It is, however, impossible to get worm bait here during the period of neap tides. I then prefer to go to Penzance, Newlyn or Mousehole where worm supplies are more plentiful.

Just off the entrance to the harbour lies a rocky reef known as the Cowloe. Although this reef acts as a partial breakwater it does break in rough weather and the consequent swells run past the harbour in to the main beach. Getting afloat and landing back on the beach in the harbour can be the most difficult parts of any trip. Although excellent dinghy fishing is to be had in the bay, safety first must always be the keyword. Foolhardy visiting anglers, who ignored local advice, have been drowned. The 'tail' of the Cowloe runs in a north easterly direction towards Aire Point and does not show until half tide. There are two leading marks on shore, behind the Old Success Hotel, which when kept in line will lead you out of the Cove clearing the rocks when travelling in a NNW direction. A series of rocks and ledges continues on the same line as the Cowloe towards Aire Point for about two thirds of the distance. Then there is clear sand until a point midway between Aire Point and Creagle, the next prominent cliff face towards Cape Cornwall. From this point right up to the Brisons there is rough bottom and shallow water which should only be fished in calm conditions.

Between the Cowloe and the main beach there is an area known as Pol-an-Dre. (Pol is Cornish for 'pool'). This area is protected from half ebb to half flood by the Cowloe Rocks. It is here that the local crabbers keep their store pots of crabs and lobsters. The bottom is rough and weedy. Between this area and the beach there are the remains of a wreck. The 'Beaumaris' was torpedoed during the First World War and beached at Sennen Cove. Her wreck interfered with the traffic of boats and the shooting of the mullet seine so it was blown up. The little that remains shows just off the beach on a very low water spring tide. It offers a good, secure anchorage at high tide, especially when the wind is off-shore. The remainder of the bottom inside the ledges previously mentioned is of clean sand all the way to Aire Point, except for one small rock situated just off Escalls Carn which is the highest point of the cliff before reaching Gwenvor Beach. At low water the bottom can easily be seen on a line from the Cowloe to Aire Point. The mean depth between this line and the main beach is less than five fathoms even at high tide.

High tide at Sennen occurs approximately fifteen minutes before the time listed in local and national papers for Newlyn. All tidal predictions are taken from the tidal observatory at Newlyn. The strongest inshore tide runs down between the end of the breakwater and the Cowloe. The channel between the Cowloe and the shore is known as 'Tribben'. It is difficult to negotiate at low water because of the weed beds. At high tide with the tide running out against the wind it is often too dangerous for small craft with outboard motors of 2½ h.p. or less. There is a second tide run across the middle of the bay which runs between the Cowloe and the large outer rock call 'The Bow'. Outside the Bow runs the main tide from the Brisons in the direction of the Longships Lighthouse off Land's End.

For eight hours out of every twelve hour period the inshore tide runs in a North to South direction from the Brisons to Land's End. The last of the ebb tide makes 'up' through Tribben as does the first of the flood. The rest of the tide flows down through.

The waters of the bay inside the five fathom line are usually gin-clear and light tackle is recommended to get the best sport from the inshore species.

Whitesand Bay offers many of the species which are taken in Mount's

Bay plus the added bonus of turbot, brill and various types of ray. Spinning with ragworm or mackerel strip in the general area around Pol-an-Dre and 'The Wreck' produces pollack and coalfish to 4½lb during the autumn months with mackerel, pollack, garfish and scad being present during the summer months as well as occasional shad and the more exotic species which come into our waters on the Golf Stream during exceptionally warm summers like the one experienced in 1976. Bottom fishing in this area over the weed beds produces specimen wrasse to over 6lbs, but it can be rather expensive on terminal tackle as they tend to run into the remains of the wreck. Ledgering on the sandy patches between the rocks, and, of course, between the wreck and the beach produces plaice and flounders on worm baits. I once 'shot' a ground line here and had 30 plaice on 40 hooks. The rocks and ledges towards Aire Point all produce pollack when spinning. However one has to take care to keep one's terminal tackle well clear of the kelp beds.

The main beach is separated from Gwenvor Beach at high water by the North Rocks. At low tide the sands stretch in an unbroken curve from the lifeboat slip in the Cove right round to Aire Point. Halfways between Sennen Cove and North rocks there is a valley between the dunes known as 'Vellan-dreath'. It is generally felt that the best ground for 'flats' is from Vellandreath northwards to Aire Point. Inside the ledges the ground is snag free except for the occasional patch of dead weed.

Turbot, ray and brill (up to 4½lbs) are taken on this ground together with plaice, flounders, dabs, gurnards, lesser spotted dogfish (although not as numerous as in Mount's Bay) and greater weavers. Great care should be taken when handling weavers because of the three poisonous spines between the head and the dorsal fin. Spinning over this ground also produces mackerel, garfish and the occasional school bass. The best part of the ground is from Aire Point back towards Escalls Carn i.e. immediately off Gwenvor Beach. This is a dangerous area, however, when there is a swell or ground sea running. It is then best left well alone. With a northerly wind and a 'down' tide one can anchor in the edge of the rough between Aire Point and Creagle and let the boat come back on to the sand. One can then ledger downtide for turbot and ray, retrieving the bait slowly back towards the boat if necessary.

Fish bait is by far the best for this area. Fresh sandeels are ideal, but thin mackerel strips are a good substitute. Although I have taken more ray at anchor, I have found that drifting over the ground has produced more turbot. Although many turbot are taken on static set lines I feel that the extra movement caused by fishing on the drift gives them the extra incentive 'to take'. Turbot have quite a large mouth when compared to the other inshore flats and often a small turbot will take a bait as long as itself. I prefer to fish here with a six foot six spinning rod; ABU 505 or 503 loaded with 9 lb.b.s.line to a single flowing trace terminating in nothing larger than a size 1/0 hook. If I am at anchor primarily for ray I use the same rod but with an old centre pin filled with heavier line. When anchoring over rough ground I use a dispensable stone kedge, but a suitable sand anchor is recommended for fishing other areas. If the wind is offshore i.e. between north east and south east, one does not want to drift too quickly over the ground or blow out to sea. The area from Creagle up to Nanquido Valley is very rough and shoal. This whole area breaks with a ground sea and should only be fished in calm conditions. Local commercial fishermen troll here for pollack with redgills and double figure fish are often taken.

A further area of sand extends from the end of Aire Point in a westerly direction and links up with a second patch in the middle of the bay. If one steams out of the Cove on the bearing marks for the Cowloe until the Bow is in line with The Peal, a large rock off Land's End, soft ground will be found. Here gurnards and dabs have been taken, together with pollack from the weedy edges. Further offshore, behind the Bow, in the main tide run, there is another patch of clean ground which has produced larger turbot over a stone in weight, specimen weavers and large ray.

Between Sennen Cove and the Longships Lighthouse lies a conspicuous rock called Shark's Fin which shows at half water. It is here that large pollack over specimen weight are taken by commercial fishermen and charter skippers. The whole area around the lighthouse produces good pollack and coalfish. The old National Records for these two species were taken here years ago before wreck fishing became popular. Near the Longships there is an area known as the Longships Sands. It is worked by commercial longliners and charter boats working out of Penzance and Newlyn. Specimen ray and turbot are taken here. However, conditions have to be perfect for dinghy anglers to fish the Longships area. It is best fished in the company of experienced local boatmen.

During the past ten years I have taken the following species from the shallow waters of the bay, both by rod and line and by set ground lines. Bass, Bogue, Brill, Coalfish, Common Topknot, Conger, Dab, Lesser Spotted Dogfish, Flounder, Garfish, Greater Weaver, Grey Gurnard, Red Gurnard, Tub Gurnard, Ling, Mackerel, Grey Mullet, Plaice, Pollack, Blonde Ray, Cuckoo Ray, Sandy Ray, Small-Eyed or Painted Ray, Scad, Twaite Shad, Trigger or File Fish, Turbot and Wrasse. Of the above named species the following were specimen fish, Bogue (1-6-3); Flounder (2-2-0); Weaver (1-6-0); Scad (1-15-2); Trigger Fish (2-6-7); Plaice (3-12-0).

The Bogue, Twaite Shad and Scad are all local Club and County Boat Caught records. The largest blonde ray taken on a set line just off the beach in 1981 weighed in at 25lbs and was taken in less than five fathoms of water. The largest turbot to be taken in this area was hooked on a set ground line and weighed 28 lbs. Many turbot taken in these inshore waters are below the minimum size as recommended by the N.F.S.A. and providing they are not too badly hooked they are returned to the water. The majority of ray taken in the past ten years have been small-eyeds, up to a maximum weight of fourteen pounds. The best small-eyed ray taken from the shore weighed in at just under twelve pounds. No thornbacks have been taken inshore as the ground is too clean for them although they are said to be taken over a patch of gravel near The Brisons. The waters off the Cove are better for turbot and ray while the more sheltered waters of Mount's Bay give the dinghy angler better sport with plaice and dabs.

Inshore Boat Fishing for Pollack in West Cornwall

Visiting dinghy owners who bring their craft on holiday to West Cornwall will find that the inshore waters around the Cornish coast offer many species during the summer months. When spinning in waters of about five fathoms or so one is likely to catch inshore pollack. Although these fish are not often taken in excess of five pounds they do give good sport on light tackle; more sport in relation to body weight than the larger fish taken from the charter boats working deep water wrecks and reefs.

Patches of mixed ground along the coast seem to offer better chances of taking pollack than the hard ground consisting of heavy kelp beds. Due to the unusual clarity of the water, sand patches, interspersed with light weedy areas, can easily be identified. Drifting along the edges of the many inshore rocks and reefs, rather than fishing over the top of them can also produce fish, although tackle losses here are likely to be greater than when fishing over mixed bottom. There are many such marks shown on the chart for the inner part of Mount's Bay, known as Penzance Bay, within the five fathom line.

Wherever possible I prefer to fish on the drift, allowing the wind and the tide to take the dinghy over the chosen mark. If conditions are not suitable for drift fishing I would anchor my dinghy up-tide of the chosen mark, cast over the stern and retrieve slowly against the tide. In this way the tide will give extra movement to the bait. When drift fishing it is not necessary to retrieve very quickly as the movement of the boat is often sufficient to move the bait and keep it clear of the bottom.

I normally use an ABU Suecia 6'6" spinning rod, together with either a 503 or 505 reel loaded with 9 lb b.s. line with a simple flowing trace about three feet in length. Hooks are usually long-shanked dab-hooks which I find more suitable for holding ragworm bait and are quite adequate for the thin mackerel strips which I often use as an alternative. I dig my own king ragworm from the designated worm digging area in Newlyn Harbour, while Mousehole Harbour has its own supply of small ragworm. I hardly ever use more than a quarter or half ounce drilled ball weight when spinning. Indeed, in calm conditions I often dispense with the weight altogether, just letting the tide carry the trace away from the boat with the weight of the swivel and bait being sufficient to take the bait to the required depth. Between Mousehole and St.Clement's Island, which lies a quarter mile off the harbour entrance, lies a small patch of sand and mixed ground between the surrounding kelp beds known as the Drethen. I have fished this spot for many years and one can always guarantee to catch pollack on light spinning tackle. Over the years I have taken many fishless visiting anglers off the local pier, where they have been using fruitless methods, out to this mark with a guarantee of catching enough pollack to satisfy their needs.

Fishing on the drift I would find the outside edge of the sand to the south and drift over it with the flood tide until I reached the inner or northern boundary. This process would be repeated with each drift covering a different line across the mark. It fishes best at anchor on the flood tide from about two hours flood up to high water. I would anchor in the kelp bed to the south side and let the boat swing back on to the edge of the sand. Casting down tide I would work in an arc from midships on the port side right round the stern to midships on the starboard side thus giving myself a 180 degree fishing area where the slowly retrieved bait would be worked against the tide. I normally let the bait sink nearly to the bottom before commencing the retrieve. With a little practice one can soon judge the depth to a fine art. One should not hurry the retrieve as many of the pollack take within a fathom of the surface, coming up under the dinghy before striking the bait. With practice one can feel the drag of the fish's mouth over the bait before feeling the bite. Often one does not need to strike as these pollack will readily take a whole king ragworm and make off with it. However, striking usually means that one can lip hook the fish making it easier to unhook those which are too small to retain for eating. The fish average 2–2½ lbs with the better specimens going to about five pounds. Although 'small-fry' compared to the double figure fish taken by the charter boats they do provide excellent sport on light tackle. One has to give a certain amount of line without letting the fish get to the bottom and judging just how much to give adds to the pleasure of the sport. On this particular mark a dozen good king ragworm would virtually guarantee a dozen pollack. I use the whole worms for spinning and when they are exhausted I use the broken pieces left over for bottom fishing for plaice, flounders or wrasse. The best catch here to three spinning rods was fifty-six pollack in two hours fishing.

A second favoured inshore mark of mine is the area off Sennen Cove known as Pol-an-Dre. My best personal catch here was 48 pollack in the same number of casts using king ragworm. I only packed up because I ran out of bait!! Over neap tides if supplies of king rag are in short supply I feather for mackerel and use the thin 'belly' strips for my spinning bait.

Record Fish from West Penwith Waters

The excellence of fishing in Penwith waters is reflected in the recently issued Record Fish Lists at both County and National levels. The Junior Record list issued by the Cornish Division of the N.F.S.A. shows that the junior members of the M.B.A.S. hold thirty-eight junior records, while the senior members of the club hold the same number of senior County Records. The Open County Record List, which is based on the record lists of both the Cornish Division of the N.F.S.A. and the C.F.S.A. shows that the senior members of the club hold twenty-three open Cornish records. Other record fish have been taken by anglers from the neighbouring clubs of St.Ives, Goldsithney, Porthleven, Camborne, Redruth and Helston.

*Junior County Record Holders
from the M.B.A.S.*

Boat

Black Bream	3-3-0	Rodney Thomas	Monk Fish	14-11-10	R. Thomas
Coalfish	16-10-0	Neil Treneer	Pollack	16-10-11	N. Treneer
Cod	17-10-0	C. Tonkin	S.E. Ray	5-0-0	M. Piantino
Dab	1-1-4	A. Sharp	Scad	1-4-1	N. Treneer
L.S. Dogfish	2-11-0	L. Piantino	Blue Shark	64-0-0	R. Thomas
Flounder	2-4-6	G. Richards	Sole	2-15-12	M. Piantino
Garfish	1-4-0	W. Moon	Triggerfish	2-3-0	S. Pender
G. Gurnard	0-14-0	M. Coward	G. Weaver	1-2-12	N. Treneer
Tub Gurnard	1-7-8	M. Coward	Ballan Wrasse	6-1-14	L. Piantino

Shore

Angler Fish	G. Rowe	10-8-0	G. Mullet	C. McClary	5-1-0
Bull Huss	C. Cripps	14-4-8	Plaice	K. Nicholls	5-6-8
Coalfish	K. Nicholls	2-2-8	Pollack	P. Nicholls	6-7-12
Cod	K. Nicholls	2-4-10	Scad	R. Whipp	1-5-8
Conger	C. Cripps	20-15-0	Sole	K. Gibbs	1-2-8
Dab	R. Whipp	1-1-3	Turbot	K. Nicholls	4-13-9
Silver Eel	J. Oxenham	2-2-0	Ballan Wrasse	K. Nicholls	6-5-15
Flounder	M. Pilcher	2-15-12	Cuckoo Wrasse	K. Nicholls	0-11-0
Garfish	P. Mainwaring	1-10-2			
Tub Gurnard	R. Whipp	1-12-9			
John Dory	K. Nicholls	1-4-0			
G.G. Mullet	J. Nicholls	1-9-0			

It is interesting to note that the Nicholls family of Newlyn share nine Junior County Records between them with Kevin Nicholls holding seven.

M.B.A.S. Senior County Record Holders

Boat

Bogue	1-6-3 S.G. Pender	Brill	10-13-7 R. Downing
Cod	36-4-0 C. James	Silver Eel	1-7-0 S. Watkins
G. Gurnard	1-2-3 S.G. Pender	S. Gurnard	0-12-0 S.G. Pender
Megrim	1-9-7 T. Jones	Opah	128-0-0 A.R. Blewett
Blonde Ray	21-6-8 L. Williams	Rockling	1-6-14 S.G. Pender
Scad	1-15-12 S.G. Pender	Allis Shad	1-4-0 C. Thomas
Porbeagle	300-0-0 J. Eathorne	Sole	2-15-12 M. Piantino(Jnr.)
Sunfish	30-0-0 R. Meek	Triggerfish	2-6-7 S.G. Pender
Turbot	28-8-0 W. Rodda	G. Weaver	1-15-14 C. Thomas
B. Wrasse	6-9-9 R. Dunn	C. Wrasse	1-15-0 R. Berry
Corkwing Wr.	0-8-0 S.G. Pender	Wreckfish	6-13-6 C. Thomas

Shore

Bass	13-8-0 W. Chiffers	Bogue	1-5-8 A. Taylor
G.H. Bream	3-9-4 G. Nicholls	Coalfish	5-5-0 D. Smith-Howell
Silver Eel	2-7-0 W. Gibson	Garfish	2-2-0 L. Chapple
G. Gurnard	1-2-8 L. Washer	John Dory	1-10-0 L. Edmonds
G.G. Mullet	1-9-0 J. Nicholls(Jnr.)	G. Mullet	5-14-0 L. Chapple
Plaice	5-6-8 K. Nicholls(Jnr.)	Pollack	12-11-0 C. Allsop
Pouting	3-14-0 T. Webb	Allis Shad	1-8-0 P. Harvey
Topknot	0-10-8 S.G. Pender	G. Weaver	1-12-0 L. Chapple

It will be noticed that some of the Junior Record holders also hold the corresponding record at Senior level for the same specie. Some of the present County Records, such as the Great Weaver caught by Les Chapple in 1961 exceed the current National record. Timmy Webb's shore caught pouting, taken from Newlyn Pier in 1972, when he was still a Junior member of the club, beat the National Record by ten ounces.

M.B.A.S. 'Open' Cornish Record Holders

Boat / Shore

Bogue	1-6-3 S.G. Pender	Bass	13-8-0 W. Chiffers
Brill	10-13-7 R. Downing	Bogue	1-5-8 A. Taylor
Cod	36-4-0 C. James	G.H. Bream	3-9-4 G. Nicholls
Silver Eel	1-7-0 S. Watkins	Silver Eel	2-7-0 W. Gibson
S. Gurnard	0-12-0 S.G. Pender	G.G. Mullet	1-9-0 J. Nicholls
Opah	128-0-0 A.R. Blewett	G. Mullet	5-14-0 L. Chapple
Sole	2-15-12 M. Piantino	Pollack	12-11-0 C. Allsop
Sunfish	30-0-0 R. Meek	Pouting	3-14-0 T. Webb
Triggerfish	2-6-7 S.G. Pender	Allis Shad	1-8-0 P. Harvey
Turbot	28-8-0 W. Rodda	Topknot	0-10-8 S.G. Pender
Cuckoo Wr.	1-15-0 R. Berry	G. Weaver	1-12-0 L. Chapple
Corkwing Wr.	0-8-0 S.G. Pender		

It is also interesting to note that a grand total of sixteen Cornish Records, nine Junior and seven Senior have been set from my own twelve foot dinghies in the past ten years. These record fish have been mainly inshore species taken from the inner areas of Mount's Bay, or just off Sennen Cove on the north coast. The County Senior/Junior joint record sole of 2-15-12 taken by Mark Piantino was also landed from my Mousehole dinghy.

Junior Records
Sole 2-15-12 M. Piantino Mousehole
Dab 1-1-4 A. Sharp Mousehole
L.Dog 2-11-0 L. Piantino Mousehole
Garfish 1-4-0 W. Moon Sennen
G. Gurnard 0-14-0 M. Coward Mousehole
Tub Gurn. 1-7-8 M. Coward Mousehole
S.E. Ray 5-0-0 M. Piantino Sennen
Trigger 2-3-0 S. Pender Sennen
Wrasse 6-1-14 L. Piantino Sennen

Senior Records
Bogue 1-6-3 Sennen
G. Gurnard 1-2-3 Mousehole
Scad 1-15-12 Sennen
Corkwing 0-8-0 Mousehole
S. Gurnard 0-12-0 Mousehole
Rockling 1-6-14 Mousehole
Trigger 2-6-7 Sennen

All the above fish were taken by myself.

M.B.A.S. Records

	Shore			Boat	
Angler Fish	18-1-0	Phil Harvey	1968 29-8-0	Alan Johns	1977
Bass	13-8-0	W. Chiffers	1962 8-10-15	M. Pilcher	1974
Bogue	1-5-8	A. Taylor	1981 1-6-3	S. Pender	1973
Bream Black	3-8-2	P. Maddern	1976 4-12-0	D.Smith/Howell	1966
Bream Red	1-15-12	L. Washer	1980 4-12-8	L. Williams	1966
Bream Gilthead	3-9-4	G. Nicholls	1982		
Brill			10-13-7	R. Downing	1970
Bull Huss	14-4-4	C. Cripps	1969 17-4-0	Mrs.B.Matthews	1969
Coalfish	5-0-0	D.Smith/Howell	1961 25-13-0	Tony Blewett	1974
Cod	5-4-5	D.Allcorn	1982 36-4-0	C. James	1975
Common Topknot	0-10-8	S. Pender	1972		
Comber			1-0-5	P. Sullivan	1979
Conger	29-9-0	W. Mainwaring	1979 50-0-0	R. Bates	1973
Dab	1-11-14	D. Allcorn	1980 1-7-0	S. Pender	1969
Eel Silver	2-7-0	W. Gibson	1959 1-7-0	S. Watkins	1979
Flounder	3-2-4	W. Gibson	1963 2-15-12	H. Knowles	1978
Garfish	2-2-0	L. Chapple	1959 1-13-8	W. Clegg	1963
Gurnard Grey	1-2-8	L. Washer	1980 1-2-3	S. Pender	1981
Gurnard Red	2-10-0	R. Powell	1974 2-13-0	K. Matthews	1969
Gurnard Tub	1-12-6	R. Whipp	1982 1-7-8	M. Coward	1979
Haddock	0-9-0	M. Jewell	1966 6-2-0	D.Smith/Howell	1967
John Dory	1-10-0	L. Edmonds	1950 5-14-7	C. Thomas	1977
Hake			10-12-0	K. Matthews	1964
Herring			0-10-8	S. Pender	1970

Species	Weight	Angler	Year	Weight	Angler	Year
L.S.Dogfish	3-0-8	M. Stange	1982	2-11-0	L. Piantino	1980
Ling	4-3-7	P. Maddern	1981	37-0-0	G. Maddern	1976
Mackerel	2-9-10	C. Keyes	1977	2-11-15	K.Goldsworthy	1975
Monkfish	18-0-0	W. Maguire	1951			
Megrim				1-9-7	T. Jones	1979
Mullet Golden	1-9-0	J. Nicholls	1979			
Mullet Grey	5-14-0	L. Chapple	1961	3-14-12	G. Nicholls	1977
Mullet Red	1-5-0	W. Gibson	1957			
Plaice	5-6-8	K. Nicholls	1980	4-8-0	S. Pender	1979
Pollack	12-11-0	C. Allsop	1960	19-6-6	M. Jones	1982
Pouting	3-14-0	T. Webb	1972	3-10-8	R. Barber	1979
Opah				128-0-0	Tony Blewett	1973
Ray Blonde	9-10-3	S. Watkins	1977	21-6-8	L. Williams	1967
Ray Small-Eyed	11-15-8	P. Maddern	1981	11-8-9	E. Lewzey	1969
Ray Thornback	4-11-0	D. Allcorn	1966	11-0-0	M. Jacobson	1964
Ray Spotted	4-6-0	P. Spry	1982			
Rockling T.B.	2-0-2	B. Friend	1966	1-6-14	S. Pender	1981
Scad	1-10-0	L. Rolfe	1962	1-15-12	S. Pender	1981
Shad Allis	1-8-0	P. Harvey	1969	1-4-0	C. Thomas	1973
Shad Twaite				1-4-0	S. Pender	1976
Shark Blue				85-0-0	N. Hargreaves	1968
Shark Porbeagle				300-0-0	J. Eathorne	1951
Spurdog	4-9-4	R. Powell	1978	13-6-0	R. Barber	1978
Sole	1-11-4	K. Gibbs	1972	2-15-12	M. Piantino	1982
Sunfish	26-5-0	M. Nicholls	1976	30-0-0	R. Meek	1962
Tope				34-0-0	Mrs.L.Clegg	1961
Trigger Fish				2-6-7	S. Pender	1976
Turbot	8-3-8	A. Perkins	1966	28-8-0	W. Rodda	1962
Weaver	1-12-0	L. Chapple	1961	1-15-14	C. Thomas	1976
Whiting	2-1-5	W.Mainwaring	1982	4-0-0	F. Johns	1967
Wrasse Ballan	6-5-12	K. Nicholls	1978	6-9-9	R. Dunn	1976
Wrasse Cuckoo	1-4-1	D. Allcorn	1974	1-15-0	R. Berry	1971
Wrasse Corkwing	0-9-0	S. Pender	1971	0-8-0	S. Pender	1971
Wreck Fish				6-13-6	C. Thomas	1975
Gurnard Streaked				0-12-0	S. Pender	1979

The following records were set in 1983.

Shore
Dab	1-15-1	J. Matthews
Red Bream	2-2-5	D. Allcorn
Conger	31-8-0	H. Knowles
S.E. Ray	13-4-0	P. Spry
Scad	1-10-8	T. Rowe

Boat
Coal Fish	26-1-0	M. Jones
L.S. Dog	2-15-14	R. Hobday
Tub Gurnard	1-8-0	S.G. Pender

Useful Information

General information regarding angling in Cornwall can be obtained from the local Tourist Information Centres, or from the local District Councils' offices. Cornwall is divided into six administrative districts. Each district publishes its own guide for visitors. The guides detail places of interest, types of accommodation available, together with sports and leisure activities. Copies of the current Penzance and District Holiday Guide are available from the Resorts Officer, Mr. E. Anstey at Penwith District Offices, St. Clare, Penzance or from the Tourist Information Centre, Alverton Street, Penzance (opposite St.John's Hall). This centre is open daily from June to September while during the period October to May it is open Monday to Friday only. The centre also operates a Tourist Accommodation Finding Service.

Visiting anglers contemplating staying in the St.Ives area should contact the Tourist Information Centre at the Guildhall, St.Ives (Tel. Penzance 796297) which is open on the same basis as the T.I.C. in Penzance. Copies of the St.Ives and District Guide are available here as well as from Penwith District Council Offices in Penzance. These districts are also responsible for the licensing of charter skippers and other boatmen. Penwith District Council offices are situated at St. Clare, Penzance at the top of St.Clare Street above West Cornwall Hospital.

Details of charter boats available are obtainable from the Council or from the advertising boards around the harbour areas both in Penzance and at St.Ives. Both pleasure and angling trips are well advertised and bookings in Penzance may be made at various shops around the dock area including the Shell Shop, Penzance Aquarium etc.

For charter trips, i.e. sharking, wrecking, reefing or feathering from Mousehole contact Frank Wallis, 2 Commercial Road, Mousehole (Phone Penzance 731 511). Anglers in the St.Ives area should contact either J.H. Paynter, 30 Bowling Green Terrace, St.Ives, (Phone Penzance 796812) or R.D. & H. Paynter, 3 Carnglaze Place, St.Ives, (Phone Penzance 795505). Angling trips are also operated from picturesque Lamorna Cove during the summer months on the 'Gay Venture' run by Mr. L.T. Roberts, 23 Holly Terrace, Heamoor, Penzance. Other charter trips are also available from the port of Hayle.

OTHER LOCAL DISTRICT OFFICE DETAILS

Kerrier District Council	Camborne 712941/714851 Helston 2921
Carrick District Council	Pydar Street, Truro 78131.
Restormel District Council	39 Penwinnick Road, St.Austell 4466.
Caradon District Council	Luxstowe House, Liskeard 43818.
North Cornwall D. Council	Priory House, Bodmin 4471.

LOCAL TACKLE SHOPS IN PENWITH

Bob Baird, 40 Fore Street, Copperhouse, Hayle	Hayle 752238
Bill Knott, Mount Haven, Marazion	Penzance 711191
Vernon Lanxon, 18 Causewayhead, Penzance	Penzance 2736
Sports and Leisure, 4 Fernlea Terrace, St.Ives	Penzance 795424
Frank Westren, Ship Chandlers, The Bridge, Newlyn	Penzance 2413
Cosalt Ltd., Harbour Road, Newlyn	Penzance 3094
Johnny Wing, The Quay Shop, 18 Quay Street, Penzance	Penzance 3397
West Cornwall Angling Centre, 25 Penpol Terrace, Hayle	Hayle 754292

FELLOW ANGLERS

If you plan to fish the Penwith District the following fellow anglers will only be too willing to pass on help and advice.

Tony Blewett	Penzance 67704	Peter Maddern	Penzance 5280
Denis Allcorn	Penzance 4045	Roy Powell	Penzance 66814
Bill Mainwaring	Penzance 66724	Robert Matthews	St Just 9788019
Sid Pender	Sennen 690	Vic Strike	Porthleven 62491
Greg Elliott	Porthleven 2897	Albert Southwell	Hayle 9753606
Roger Calfe	Penzance 9710180		

The local Mount's Bay Angling Society (M.B.A.S.) has its Headquarters at the Dolphin Inn, near Newlyn Bridge. The committee meets on the first Tuesday in each month. The remaining Tuesday nights are open club nights. Meetings commence at 7.30 pm and visiting anglers are welcome to come along and meet club members. The club also runs a very successful Annual Fishing Festival in August each year with many of the impressive trophies and awards being available to visiting anglers.

ACCOMMODATION

'The West Country' and 'Where to stay in the West Country' costs £1.25 post paid, from the West Country Tourist Board, Trinity House, Southernhay East, Exeter, Devon. For Cornwall County Council's Official Holiday Guide, send 60p postage, plus 35p for the Approved Accommodation Register, both available from the Cornwall Tourist Board; Dept DE, County Hall, Station Road, Truro, Cornwall TR1 3HD.

BOAT PROPRIETORS AND HIRERS

Allen J.J. Takapuna, Rosudgeon, Penzance	Germoe 3332
Custom House Quay (Falmouth) Boat Owners Ass.	Falmouth 311434
Jenkin, A. St. Anthony	Manaccan 357
Millendreath Marine Co. Ltd. Millendreath	Looe 3003
Mylor Boat Hire, Mylor Churchtown, Falmouth	Penryn 74830
Paynter J.H. 30 Bowling Green Tce., St.Ives	Penzance 796812
Paynter R.D. & H. 3 Carnglaze Place, St. Ives	Penzance 795505
Pill G.H. 106 Acacia Road, Falmouth	Falmouth 313587
Roberts J. & P.P. 19 Cardwen, Pelynt	Lanreath 418
Roberts K.S. 27 Penoweth, Mylor Bridge	Penryn 74037
Sea Boat Services Ltd. Arwenack St., Falmouth	Falmouth 313808
Seawest, 19 Gerrans Hill	Portscatho 649
Tomlin, W.J. West Street	Polruan 235

CHARTER TRIPS

M.V. Philanderer, Sea Safaris Ltd., Higher Penjerrick, Falmouth or phone Colin MacGillvray 0326 250711
60ft Monkswood, Frank Vinnicombe, Mylor, Falmouth Penryn 72775
Sealand Holidays Ltd., 26 Trefusis Road, Flushing or 01 570 3628
M.V. Excalibur, Mevagissey, Tel St.Austell 0726 882214
'Selachian', Padstow, shark and bottom fishing Padstow 0841 532241
Valency, Ken Townley, Fowey 3322

FISHERMEN

Arthur A.G. 1 Arheim Terrace, Flushing Penryn 74807
Curtis, Robert, Lower Lanhay Farmhouse, Gerrans, Portscatho 505
May, A.J. 24 Silvershell Road, Port Isaac 716
Vinnicombe, Robin, 9 Arwenack Avenue, Falmouth 314810
Wallis, Frank, 2 Commercial Road, Penzance 731 511

TACKLE SHOPS IN AREAS OTHER THAN PENWITH

Angling Centre, 10a Victoria Place   St.Austell 63377
Bill's Tackle Box, 34 Arwenack Street   Falmouth 315849
Jack Bray, The Quay, Looe   Looe 2504
Burton, L.A. The Rod and Line, Little Green   Polperro 72361
Central Sports, 2 Crantock Street, Newquay   Newquay 4101
Helston Sports, 6 Wendron Street, Helston   Helston 2097
Key R.E. Quay Garage, Quay Road, St.Agnes   St.Agnes 2217
Langdon, J. 20 St.Mary's Street, Truro   Truro 2207
Len's Angling Centre, 93 Killigrew Street   Falmouth 318636
Mevagissey Shark Angling Centre, West Wharf   Mevagissey 3430
Noakes H.M. 6 Fore Street, Mevagissey   Mevagissey 3310
One and All Sports, 39 Fore Street   Redruth 216988

Polperro: Mr L.A. Burton, The Rod and Line, Little Green   0503 72361
Reid James, 10 The Esplanade, Fowey   Fowey 2207
Shark Fishing Agent, F. Hoskin, East Looe Quay   Looe 2189
City Angling Centre, Peoples Palace, Pydar St. Truro. (0872 75340)
The Tackle Box, 13 Fore Street, Mevagissey   Mevagissey 3513
The Tackle Box, 11 Trinity Street, St.Austell   St.Austell 5114
Transatlantic Fishing Systems Ltd. Eastwood Road   Penryn 74024

SEA ANGLING CLUBS AFFILIATED TO THE N.F.S.A.(CORNISH DIVISION)
(Details kindly provided by Tony Blewett, Hon. Sec. of the Cornish Division of the N.F.S.A.)

Callington S.A.C.	Hon.Sec.R. May	Stoke Road, Kelly Bray, Callington
Camelford & Dist.	Hon.Sec.P. Davey	4 Victoria Road, Camelford
Camborne A.A.	Hon.Sec.C.J.Goldsworthy	10 Pentalek Road, Camborne
Clinton Arms S.A.C.	Hon.Sec.R.T. Moyle	52 Raymond Road, Redruth
Cubert S.A.C.	Hon.Sec.B. Hocking	7 Lamanva Road, Illogan, Redruth
Culdrose S.A.C.	Hon.Sec.C.P.O. MacDonald	c/o Pay Office, R.N.A.S. Culdrose, Helston
E.S.S.A. S.A.C.	Hon.Sec.J.C. Webber	2 Rashleigh Avenue, St.Stephens, Saltash
E.C.C.Ports S.A.C.	Hon.Sec.F.C.P. Hellyer	c/o E.C.C. Ports Ltd., Harbour Office, Par.
Fowey S.A.C.	Hon.Sec.Mrs.P.Shelley	'Castledore', Tywardreath, Par.
Goldsithney S.A.C.	Hon.Sec.R. Calfe	23 St.Aubyn's, Goldsithney, Penzance
Hayle S.A.C.	Hon.Sec.A. Southwell	Telephone Hayle 9753606.
Helston & Dist. S.A.C.	Hon.Sec.J. Maundrill	Long Reach, Ruan Minor, Helston.
Heathcoats S.A.C.	Hon.Sec.F. Williams	55 Cathebedron Road, Carnhell Green, Camborne.
Herbert A.C.	Hon.Sec.H. Saunders	'Avalon', Hallan Moor, Lanner.
Helston R.B.L. S.A.C.	Hon.Sec.M. Jennings	Tanyard Lane, Helston.
Holmans S.A.C.	Hon.Sec.P. Lanyon	60 Rosemellin, Camborne.

Looe S.A.C.	Hon.Sec.D. Snell	'Sunnybank', Trewidland, Liskeard.
Launceston S.A.C.	Hon. Sec. L.H. Harrison	47 St.Leonard's Road, Lanstephen, Launceston.
Liskeard & Dist. S.A.C.	Hon. Sec. J. Goulding	1 Tripp Hill, St.Neot, Liskeard.
Mount's Bay A.S.	Hon.Sec.D.J. Cains	37 Treassowe Road, Penzance.
Mevagissey S.A.C.	Hon.Sec.G.E.M. Stuart	1 Lower Well Park, Polkirt Hill, Mevagissey.
Newquay R.B.L. S.A.C.	Hon.Sec.R. Addison	6 Stanways Road, Newquay.
Perranporth S.A.C.	Hon.Sec.A.D. Naylor	16 Tregunda Road, Perranporth.
Porthleven S.A.C.	Hon.Sec.D. Ward	43 St.Peter's Way, Porthleven.
Red Lion S.A.C.	Hon.Sec.D.E. Wood	c/o The Red Lion, Helston.
Redruth S.A.A.	Hon.Sec.Mrs.L.Cockerill	Flat 1 Paynter's Lane End, Illogan, Redruth.
Rame Peninsula S.A.C.	Hon.Sec.P. Carne	100 West Street, Millbrook, Torpoint
Railway Inn S.A.C.	Hon.Sec.M. Bawden	5 Trevean Close, Treseithin, Camborne.
S.W.E.B. S.A.C.	Hon.Sec.D. Simpson	S.W.E.B. Admin. Dept.; Pool, Redruth.
St.Ives A.S.	Hon.Sec.M. Gilbert	Sports & Leisure, St.Ives.
Truro City S.A.C.	Hon.Sec.Mrs.C.L.Cofer	22 Treverbyn Road, Truro.
Truro Post Office Social & Sports Club	Hon.Sec.B. Taylor	13 Polruan Road, Malpas Estate, Truro.
Western Excavating A.C.	Hon.Sec.G. Read	11 Halimote Road, St. Dennis.
Volunteer S.A.C.	Hon.Sec.G.R. Eley	56 Dennis Road, Liskeard.
Veor S.A.C.	Hon.Sec.G. Thomas	'Shemara', Penware Parc, Camborne.
Raleigh S.A.C.	Hon.Sec.D.G. Livick	9 Coombe Park, Cawsand.
Tintagel S.A.C.	Hon.Sec.N. Rundle	King Arthur's Castle Hotel, Tintagel.

Captions to the following illustrations are on pp. 41/2.

1

2

3

4

5

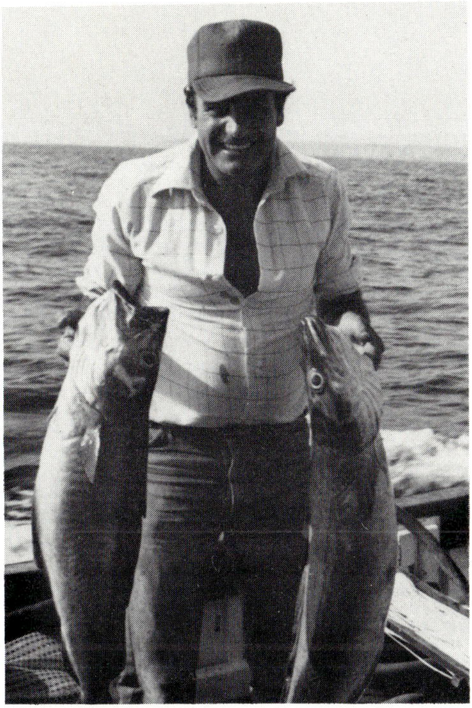

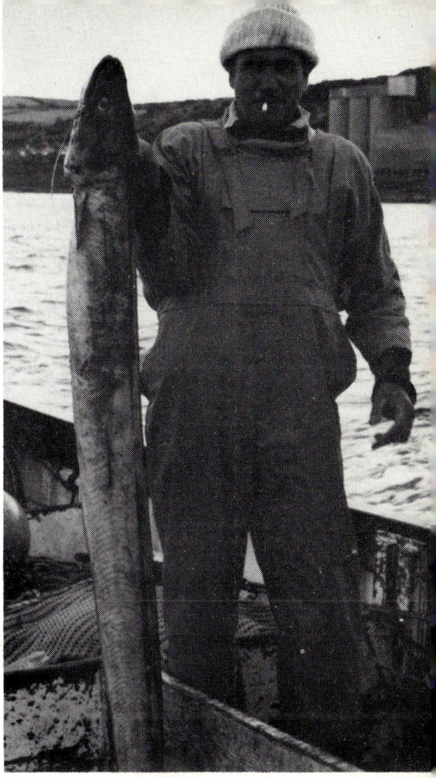

7

6

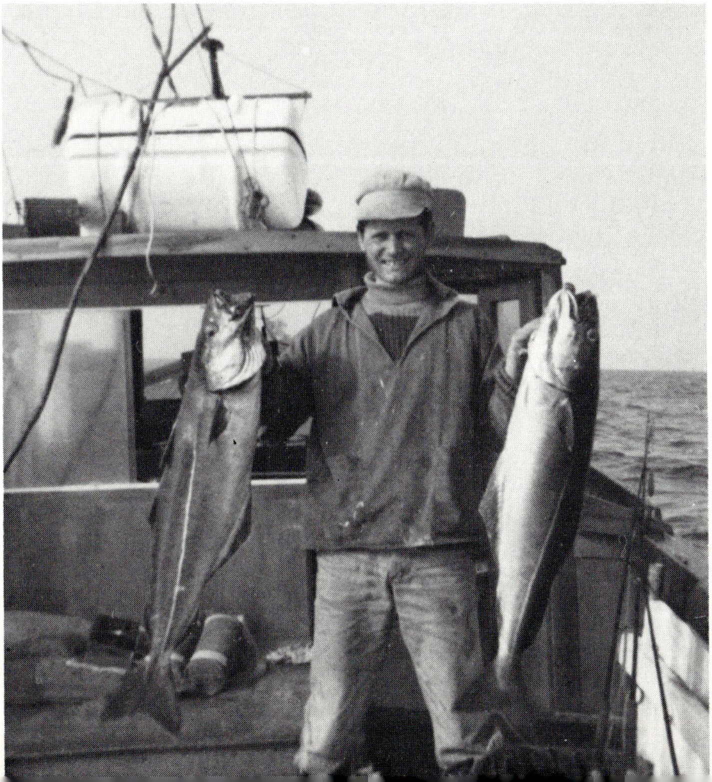

8

9

10

11

12

13

14

15

16

17

19

18

20

21

22

23

24

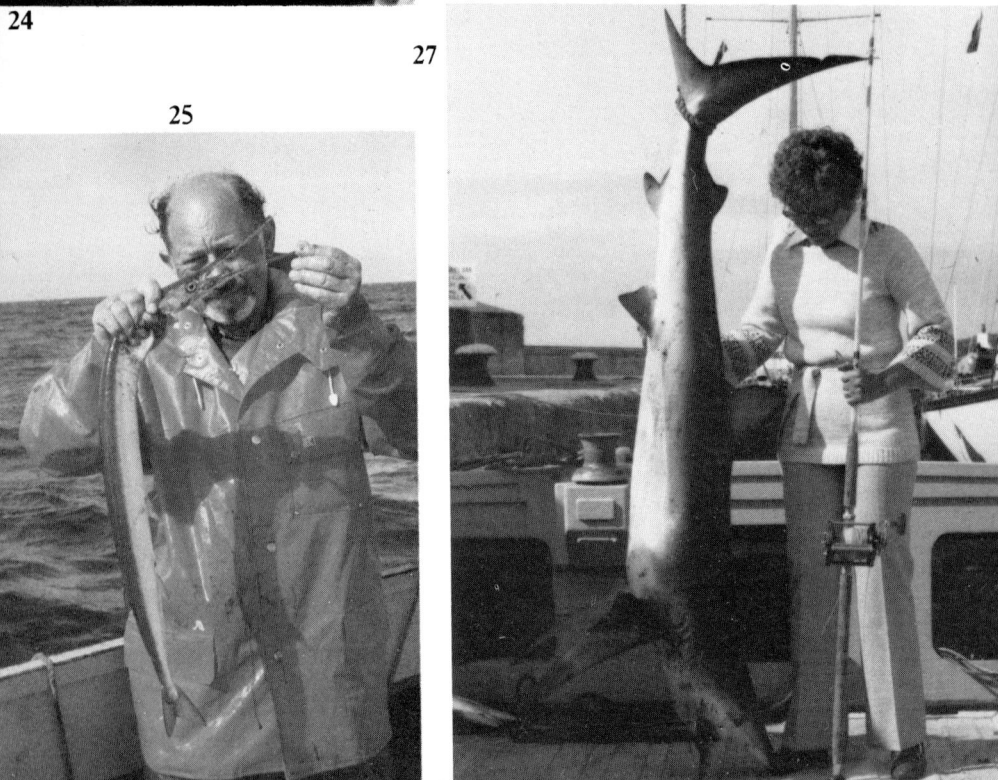

25

26

27

Captions to the illustrations on the preceding eight pages

1 Members of the Mount's Bay Angling Society with a mixed catch of fish taken on an inshore mark in Mount's Bay from the 'Lady Kathryn', skipper Peter Tonkin.

2 Three happy anglers returning to Falmouth having fished the area between the 'Manacles' and Coverack. From left to right:- J. Stoddern with a pollack of nearly 12lbs and a spotted ray; R. Moyle with a thornback ray and a hake of 8 lbs (both anglers members of the Railway Angling Club); Albert Southwell, Hon. Sec. of the Hayle Sea Angling Club with two ling of 19lbs and 17lbs. They were fishing from the M.V. Vera out of Mylor, skippered by Pat Bagnell.

3 Tony Blewett, former Chairman of the M.B.A.S. and Secretary of the Cornish Division N.F.S.A. playing his club record coalfish of 25-13-0.

4 The 'Talisman' entering Mousehole Harbour at the end of a sharking trip. The flags show that four sharks were caught that day.

5 Roy Powell, team captain of the M.B.A.S. with a pollack and ling taken from a mark in Mount's Bay from the 'Lady Kathryn'.

6 Nicky Morse of Penzance with two fine coalfish of 23½lbs and 24½lbs taken from the Lady Kathryn in August 1980 at a mark ten miles south of Newlyn. Tackle, Rod, fibretube 30lb class; 30lb b.s. line; Reel-Ambassadeur 7000. The fish were taken on redgills and won Nicky the E.F.S.A. 'Fish of the Month' Award. Skipper was again Peter Tonkin.

7 Roy Powell with a 35½ lb conger from an inshore mark in Mount's Bay.

8 Luke Piantino with an inshore plaice taken on 'The Drethen', a small sand patch just off Mousehole Harbour which also yielded his brother's record common sole.

9 A trio of happy dinghy anglers, although the catch was not very good. Sid Pender, Luke Piantino and Mark Piantino with a few wrasse taken on rough ground just off St.Clement's Island, Mousehole.

10 Luke Piantino with better quality plaice and turbot taken from the area off Aire Point which is also a noted shore mark for turbot and ray.

11 Mark Piantino with two nice pouting of 2-4-0 and 2-6-4 taken from my dinghy while fishing a mark S.E. of Mousehole Island known as 'Gallymadden'.

12 Sid Pender and Luke Piantino with a selection from a catch of over two dozen dabs taken from a mark about a quarter of a mile to the east of Mousehole in Mount's Bay.

13 Tony Blewett pictured on the North Pier at Newlyn with his club record coalfish of 25-13-0.

14 Sid Pender with his record boat-caught scad of 1-15-2 taken from the mark known as Pol-an-dre in Whitesand Bay while spinning for pollack.

15 Mark Piantino with two small inshore ray taken from Whitesand Bay in the area between Aire Point and Vellandreath.

16 Mr L. Nardini of London with his British Record garfish of 3-2-0 taken on a charter trip out of Penzance.

17 Sid Pender receiving the J. Eathorne Trophy for the best fish taken in the M.B.A.S. Annual Fishing Festival 1981.

18 Tony Blewett with his British Record opah of 128lbs taken on a charter trip in Mount's Bay.

19 Clive James of Newlyn with his club record boat-caught cod of 36-4-0.

20 Sid Pender receiving the Clifford Cory Cup for the best overall specimen taken during the club year 1980–1981 for a boat-caught scad of 1-15-2 which rated 196% of the club and N.F.S.A. specimen weight.

21 View of the British Airways helicopter and heliport at the Eastern Green, Penzance. Photograph by courtesy of British Airways.

22 Sid Pender dinghy fishing inshore Scillonian waters watching the Scillonian on her return journey to Penzance, while waiting for a bite.

23 An example of the conger available in the waters around the Isles of Scilly. Conger feed better at night. Notice also the wire trace which is recommended when fishing for the specie.

24 Two fine Scillonian ling photographed against a backdrop of some of the smaller uninhabited islands in the group.

25 A fine garfish taken from Scillonian waters by an angler fishing from John Poynter's 35ft diesel catamaran 'White Hope'.

26 Two fine pollack typical of the sport available around the Isles of Scilly. Picture taken in St.Mary's Harbour with Porthloo in the background.

27 A fine example of the quality of the shark fishing available around the Isles of Scilly. Photograph taken aboard John Poynter's 'White Hope' in St.Mary's Harbour.

4 Boat Fishing in the Isles of Scilly

Introduction

The original script of this section was written while I was living on St. Mary's, Isles of Scilly, in the summer of 1967. At the time I was a teacher at Carn Thomas School and had reached the end of four happy years on the islands. Coming from a long-established Cornish fishing family from Mousehole naturally gave me a profound interest in the sea and over the years my interest in sea angling has grown deeper as my experience has developed.

Living in Scilly gave me the first opportunity of fishing all year round since my boyhood days. Shore fishing on Scilly can be carried out all year round by the dedicated shore angler, although weather conditions usually determine when the small-boat angler can get afloat. The usual small-boat season can normally be expected to last from April through to October, with advantage being taken of the odd fine day during the winter months. The cream of inshore and deep sea fishing is found during the late summer and early autumn so that the visiting angler who comes during the late 'season' should experience the sport at its best.

During my four years on St.Mary's I was able to fish the inshore waters from my own dinghy. Although most of my dinghy fishing was carried out from St.Mary's Harbour in 'The Roads' and 'The Sound', I did take my small boat across to Porthcressa for one summer period and also fished one winter out of Watermill on the N.E. side of St.Mary's.

The notes and suggestions in the text on 'Inshore Fishing' are based on my own personal written records and experiences over the four years spent dinghy fishing in and around the islands. The notes on deep sea angling were based on information provided by the following Scillonians to whom I am deeply indebted. Without their generous help the first hand information in this section would have been very thin indeed.

Richard Lethbridge; Lou Hichens; Joe Hicks; Jimmy Williams; Mike Hicks; John Poynter; Paddy Daly; Ronald Simons; Reggie Phillips; Lloyd Hicks; Verney Thompson; Eric Guy, John Ozard and Mr Sissam.

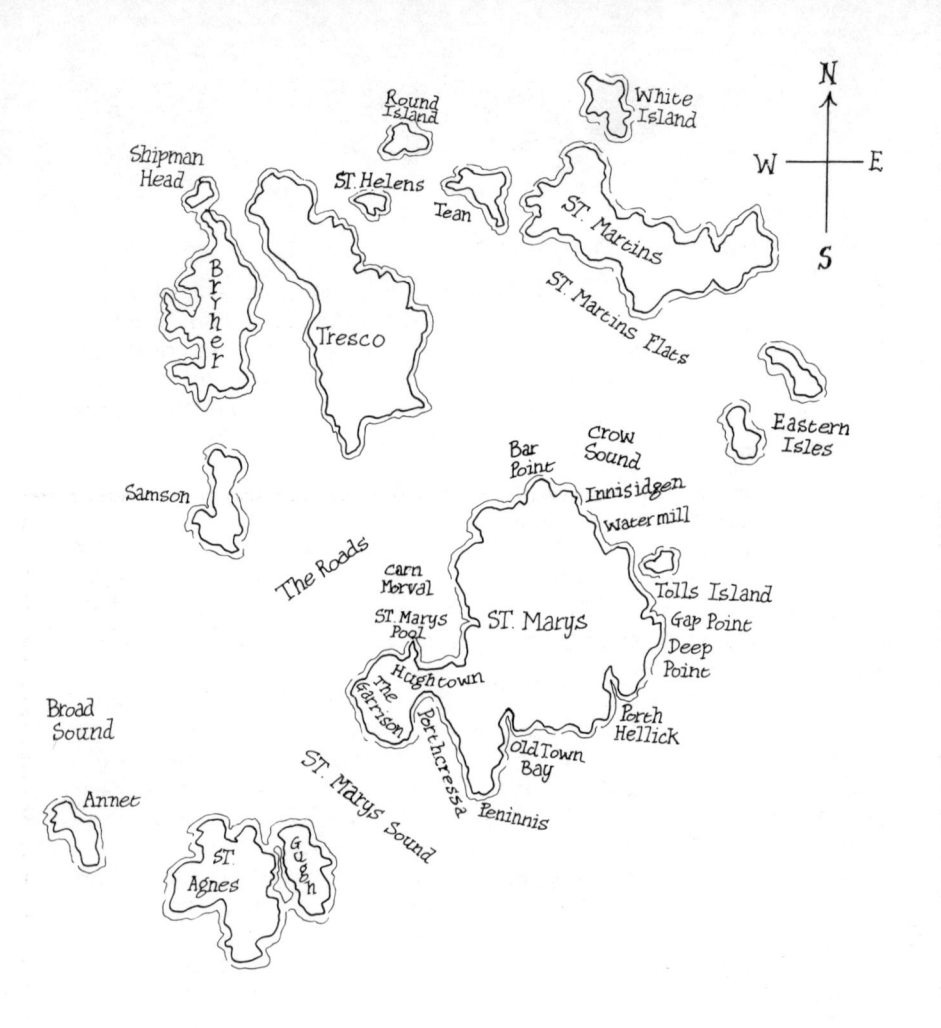

Sketch map showing the main Scilly Islands

The text has been up-dated as well as many of the statistics given from N.F.S.A. or national record sources.

The initial book 'Sea Angling in the Isles of Scilly' by Graeme Pullen has already been published and I strongly recommend any visiting angler contemplating shark fishing in Scilly to read his article on the subject as it is well written and technically very sound, although his other comments on sea fishing within the islands are rather generalised.

May I wish all visiting anglers and holiday makers who 'go down to the sea to fish', whether in their own small boats or on charter craft – 'Tight Lines'.

Inshore Boat Fishing in the Isles of Scilly

The Isles of Scilly are a group of numerous small islands lying about twenty-six miles almost due west of Land's End. The main island of St.Mary's is surrounded on three sides by the other, smaller inhabited islands of St.Martin's, Tresco, Bryher and St.Agnes. Besides the inhabited off-islands there are numerous smaller islands and islets making up the archipelago.

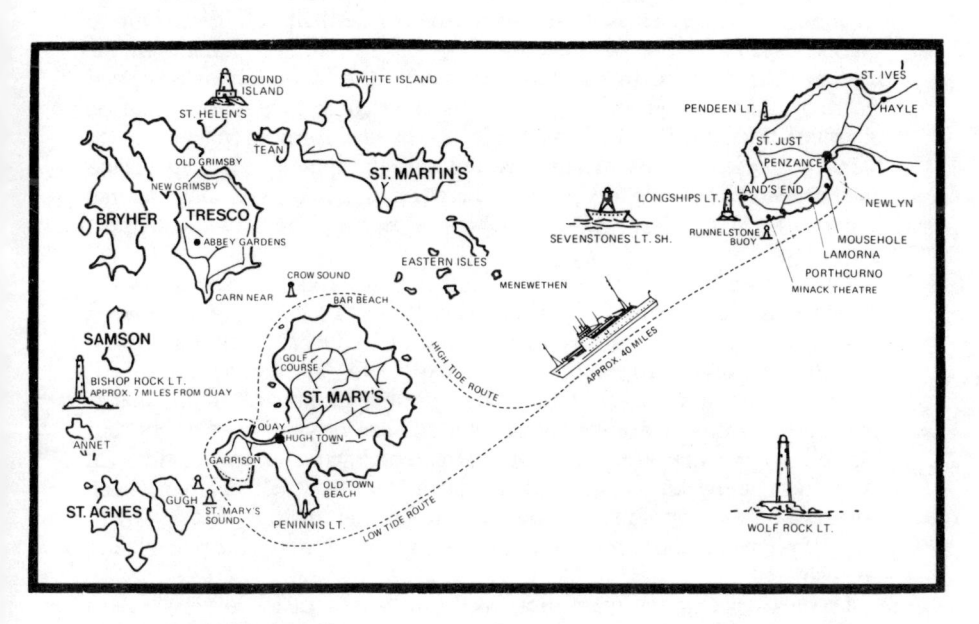

Map showing the sea journey to the Isles of Scilly, supplied by the Isles of Scilly Steamship Company Ltd.

There are regular helicopter and steamer services to St.Mary's from Penzance, Cornwall. Inter-island communication is by local launches run by the Steamship Company and by the St.Mary's Boatmen's Association. There is a holiday coach service on St.Mary's as well as mini-bus and taxi hire. However visitors are not encouraged to take their own vehicles to the islands.

There are perhaps just two classes of visitors who are likely to bring their own boats on holiday to Scilly. There will be those who are on a cruise in a cruiser, yacht or perhaps a converted M.F.V. besides those who may bring an inflatable; glass-fibre or light-weight wooden dinghy across on the steamer. Because of the restriction of cargo/deck space on the Scillonian such boats are not likely to exceed sixteen feet in length. Add to these the holiday anglers who appear each year rod in hand, and to them all I would offer a few suggestions on fishing the inshore waters in and around the Isles of Scilly. Any visiting boat owner/angler would be expected to have the necessary charts for Scillonian waters together with a copy of the local tide-tables.

Within the islands the water is comparatively shallow and depths do not often exceed nine fathoms. It is within these sheltered waters that I would recommend visiting small boat anglers to confine their activities. Due to the exceptional clarity of the water it is possible to see changes in the bottom in depths up to five fathoms except after a period of unsettled weather and heavy ground sea. Patches of weed, rock and sand can be distinguished on the seabed practically all the way from St.Mary's pier to Samson, Tresco, and St.Martin's as well as in the channel between Tresco and Bryher. The only deep water between the islands is the channel between St.Mary's and St.Agnes which is used by the steamer at most states of tide.

The sandy patches between the islands will offer various species of flat fish such as plaice, dabs, turbot, ray as well as dogfish and light-coloured wrasse feeding near the edges of the weed beds. Over the rough ground and the numerous ledges one would expect to take pollack, coalfish, bream, wrasse and conger. During the summer months of course mackerel, garfish and scad are widely distributed over varying types of bottom. Plaice have been speared by local boatmen at low water spring tides on 'The Flats' between Tresco and St.Martin's while small ray have been observed on the bottom south west of Nut Rock at low tide. Marks worth trying for flats are numerous, as are the hard ground marks for pollack and coalfish etc.

The two species of bream most likely to be caught in South Western waters are the Red Bream and the Black Bream, although Gilthead Bream and Ray's Bream have all been taken off the Cornish coast and off the islands. Sea bream are shoaling fish and once a shoal has been located sport is likely to be fast and furious. To get the best sport out of bream fishing one should use as light a tackle as conditions will permit. Adult bream are taken on baited feathers commercially while their smaller brethren prefer natural baits such as small pieces of fish bait, i.e. mackerel or garfish or launce; lugworm, ragworm, shellfish such as limpets and winkles as well as small pieces of their own species. Bream are caught at varying depths

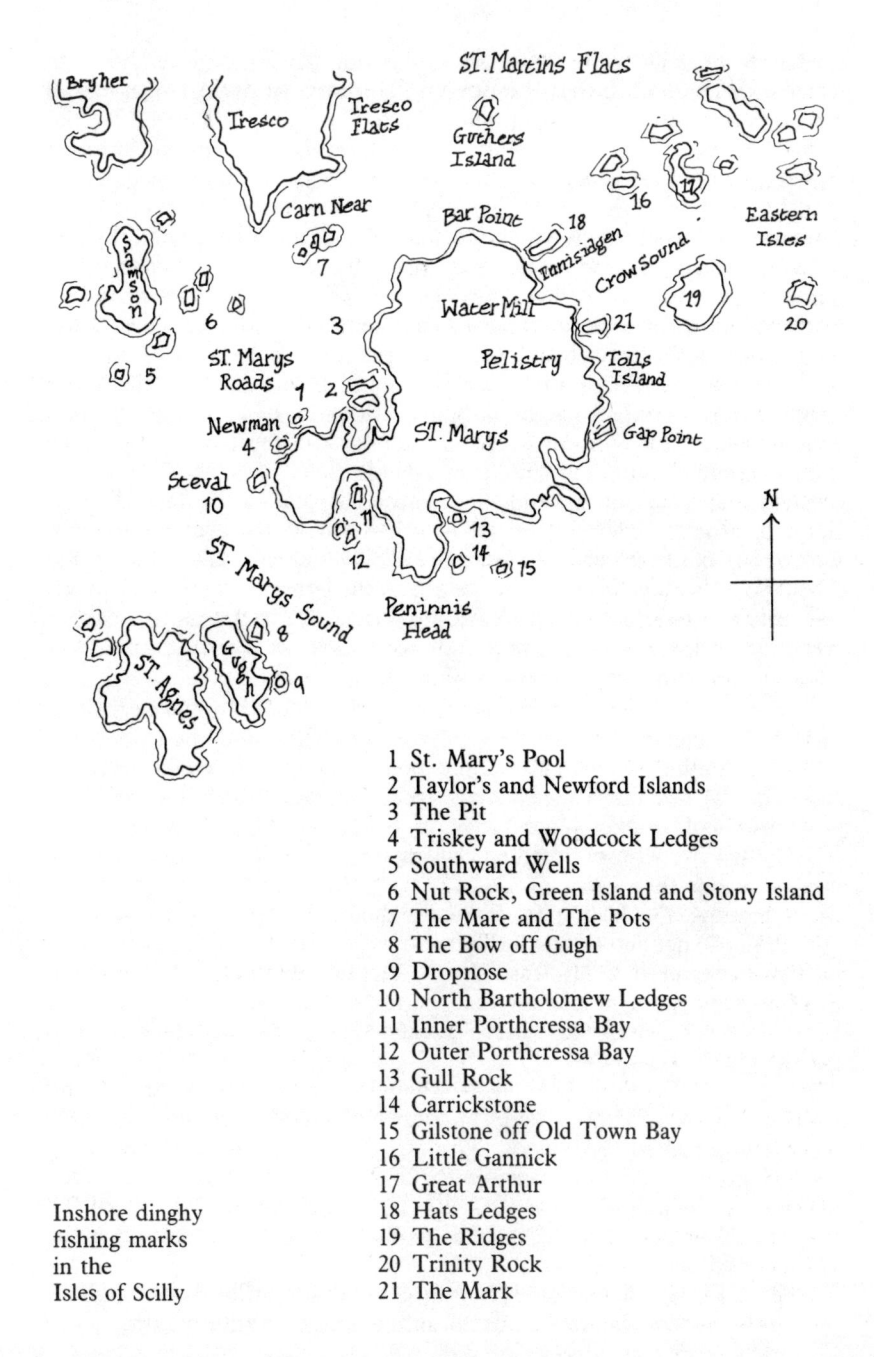

1 St. Mary's Pool
2 Taylor's and Newford Islands
3 The Pit
4 Triskey and Woodcock Ledges
5 Southward Wells
6 Nut Rock, Green Island and Stony Island
7 The Mare and The Pots
8 The Bow off Gugh
9 Dropnose
10 North Bartholomew Ledges
11 Inner Porthcressa Bay
12 Outer Porthcressa Bay
13 Gull Rock
14 Carrickstone
15 Gilstone off Old Town Bay
16 Little Gannick
17 Great Arthur
18 Hats Ledges
19 The Ridges
20 Trinity Rock
21 The Mark

Inshore dinghy
fishing marks
in the
Isles of Scilly

usually feeding higher in the water as the light begins to fade.

Over soft ground the lesser spotted dogfish is the most likely member of the dogfish family to be caught, while fishing over rough or mixed ground will produce the much larger Bull Huss. I once netted a Bull Huss of over thirteen pounds in shallow water just off Porthloo Beach which had choked itself to death on a salmon peal.

Pollack and coalfish are taken when dinghy fishing over practically any patch of rough ground or around many ledges situated between the islands. The usual run of fish between the islands would be up to six pounds with the average at about three pounds. Not so many coalfish are caught during the summer months as in the autumn as they are primarily a cold water specie. Practically every ledge on Scilly has its own pollack and it is the most common specie on Scilly. Although double-figure fish are caught around the Western Rocks and the back of the Eastern Isles they are not often encountered within the islands.

Any patch of rough ground, even those adjacent to the shore line, is likely to produce black conger when fished during the evening or night with fresh mackerel bait. One can generally expect conger within the 20–40 pounds range in inshore waters with the larger specimens frequenting reefs and wrecks in deeper offshore waters. A few years ago a conger weighing 38 lbs was caught in a crab pot which had been set just a few yards off the end of the lifeboat slip in St.Mary's Harbour.

On Scilly dabs are not as widely distributed as plaice but make excellent eating. The average size taken on light ledger tackle would be from half a pound up to the specimen size of one pound. Dabs readily take both fish baits and worm baits. Plaice have a strong preference for lugworms.

Garfish and mackerel are likely to be caught practically anywhere during the summer months when chasing the 'fry' on which they feed. On rare occasions they even invade St.Mary's harbour. Areas of tidal flow often produce the best sport but care should be taken to ensure that conditions do not deteriorate if the tide turns against the wind. I once took eighty mackerel just off Carn Near, the nearest point of Tresco to St.Mary's, in water so shallow that the top two feathers were still in the boat. However, I prefer to spin for mackerel and garfish with fine tackle to get the maximum sport.

Pouting are likely to be taken when ledgering over rough ground inshore. The pouting does not put up much of a fight, even on light tackle when compared to the bream. They tend to lie across the tide when hooked and present steady drag on the line. They often surface downtide of the boat and wallow on the surface before being retrieved. Like pollack they should be gutted and cleaned as soon as possible before eating as the gut tends to taint the flesh.

The scad, or horse mackerel, is quite commonly distributed throughout the south western waters during the summer and autumn months. They are often caught when spinning for mackerel. Scad give good sport on light tackle. Care should be taken when handling them because of the sharp serrations along the tail.

Whiting are also likely to be caught when fishing over clean ground in inshore waters. During the summer months they tend to be on the small side with the better specimens being taken during the winter. Small whiting are voracious feeders and tend to ruin the sport for other species.

GENERAL COMMENTS ON INSHORE FISHING The following species are more likely to be taken on worm baits:-
Bream, coalfish, pollack, dab, garfish, mackerel, whiting, sole, scad, plaice and wrasse. Ragworm on spinning tackle would account for coalfish, pollack, garfish, mackerel and scad while lugworm fished on or near the bottom would take bream, dabs, whiting, sole, plaice, wrasse and dogfish. Spinning with fish baits, i.e. launce or mackerel strip would probably produce coalfish, pollack, garfish, mackerel and scad while ledgering with the same type of bait should produce bream, dabs, whiting, dogfish, conger, turbot, ray and brill. Artificial sandeels and redgills of course will take pollack and coalfish while three feathers worked on the sink and draw principle are likely to result in bream, coalfish, pollack, garfish, mackerel and occasionally whiting and large wrasse being brought to the boat. Fishing from a drifting boat, providing wind and tidal conditions are suitable, would be best for coalfish, pollack, garfish, mackerel, scad, whiting, ray, turbot and brill. If conditions are not conducive to drift fishing the following species can also be taken while at anchor, i.e. bream, dab, sole, wrasse, plaice, whiting, turbot, brill, ray conger and dogfish. Turbot and brill are best taken on fish bait on the move while plaice and dabs are best taken on worm bait when at anchor. Pollack and coalfish readily take feathers worked from a drifting boat but care must be taken not to foul the bottom when drifting over the ledges. Trolling for pollack is another effective method when the water is too shallow to use (say) three feathers. When ledgering for conger never use more lead than is necessary to hold the bottom.

BAITS Natural baits are available on all Scillonian islands. Lugworm may be dug on most beaches where there is sufficient depth of sand. Recommended spots on St.Mary's include the west end of Porthcressa Beach, the eastern end of Town Beach, Porthmellon, Porthloo, Pendrathen and Bar Beach, Porth Hellick and Old Town Bay. On Scilly ragworm are known as 'rock-worm' as they are found under the stones on the sides of most beaches. They grow up to six inches in length and are considered to be superior to lugworm. As they are much more difficult to obtain I would suggest that they be kept for spinning while the lugs are used for ledgering. Spring tides are usually most productive for rockworm although they can be found on neap tides with some difficulty. Recommended areas for digging rockworm are the side of the beaches were one would also dig lugworms. White ragworm may also be dug in the harbour on St.Mary's but only on a spring tide in excess of eighteen feet. On a big tide the flat harbour bed is exposed and the whiteworm are to be found underneath the beds of sedge weed. The eastern side near the lifeboat slip seems to be the most productive. Whiteworm are excellent bait for pollack, mackerel, garfish and scad when fished on the move. It is also possible to net prawns in the harbour and a good supply of shrimps may be obtained from the many rock pools. A baited dropnet may be worked off the pier if necessary. Sandeels (launce) are not available in any quantity on the islands so that the best all-round bait for the more predatory species would be thin, fine strips of mackerel. During the summer months pleasure boat operators run evening feathering trips for holidaymakers and there are usually a few boxes of mackerel left on the pier after such trips which will provide sufficient bait for a couple of days. Of course the visiting small-boat owner can always catch his own! My own preference when fishing shallow inshore waters from a dinghy is to use as many natural baits as possible. Visiting boat owner anglers who perhaps may not wish to dig for worms etc should remember that artificial baits must be kept on the move to be successful. Some tackle and a small selection of artificial baits may be purchased from two shops on St.Mary's.

SUGGESTED FISHING AREAS   Where to fish from a small boat in Scilly is determined simply by the prevailing weather conditions at the time. In such an archipelago of islands there is always a lee shore which will give sheltered water to the small-boat angler. When the weather is settled of course the choice is open. St.Mary's Pool, which is the name given to the outer anchorage off the harbour holds several ledges and clear patches of ground which will produce pollack and plaice as well as other fish. Between Newford and Taylor's Islands, off Porthloo beach there are two patches of sand which would be worth trying with the wind between North and East providing there was no swell coming in from the westward. Just off Carn Morval, with the Daymark on St.Martin's just open of Halangy Point there is another mark known simply as 'The Pit'. A cross bearing for this mark is to line up the white patch on the old quay with the end of the main pier.

In St.Mary's Roads there are three ledges comprising the Triskey and Woodcock Ledges, the latter having two heads. These ledges lie NW of Star Castle on the Garrison and produce good pollack. Both these ledges fish well from half flood up but should not be fished with a fresh wind between SW and NW. It is an old local mark for bream.

Off the southern end of Samson lie many rocks and ledges known collectively as Southward Wells. Three anglers once took two hundred pollack and coalfish here on feathered traces, the fish being up to eight pounds in weight. Do not visit this area with the wind between E and SE as you would have a long wet haul back to St.Mary's. There are three other marks in St.Mary's Roads worth trying, along the northern side of the Roads, sheltered from NW-N winds by the islands of Samson, Bryher and Tresco. Nut Rock is easily discernable from St.Mary's harbour. It lies east of Samson, having between it and Samson, Green Island and Stony Island. The latter is reputed to be the best spot in Scilly for ragworm. Nut Rock best fishes for pollack from three quarters flood until one hour's ebb. Big wrasse are also taken in a 'hole' off the SE corner of the rock.

The Mare and the Pots lie just off Tresco, although when viewed from St.Mary's the Mare looks more like a 'frog'. Here the water is very shallow and these ledges are best fished with fine tackle on the drift at the top of a high spring tide. Between Nut Rock and the Mare there are two other small ledges where pollack and mackerel have also been taken on top tides.

On the far side of St.Mary's Sound lies the island of Gugh which is joined to St.Agnes by a sandbar at low water. Along the side of Gugh facing St.Mary's there are many rocks and ledges which in quiet weather produce middle weight pollack taken on the drift. These ledges are best fished over high water slack. The best drift is from the Bow, a large rock off Gugh, to Dropnose, the SE corner of Gugh. The North Bartholomew Ledge, marked by the Bartholomew Buoy is separated from the South Bartholomew by a channel showing seven fathom. Pollack and coalfish are taken here, preferably on the drift over high water slack. Several large wrasse have also been taken here on a feathered trace.

Porthcressa Bay to the south of Hugh Town offers mixed fishing for the small-boat angler. There is a good sand patch between the Brow and the Garrison shore which is visible from the shore at low water. From half flood onwards in good weather it is a good spot for plaice. The sand continues seaward through the channel. Pollack will be taken over rough patches and around the ledges. Good wrasse are also taken here. The sandy areas of the outer part of the bay have produced good turbot and ray while the inner area is one of the better inshore spots for plaice.

Off Old Town Bay there are various ledges, some show and break at half water, while others only break in bad weather. In the narrow entrance to the inner bay there is the conspicuous Gull Rock bisecting the channel. Small craft can easily pass either side of it although it is not easy to enter or to leave this bay at low water as the thongs form a barrier right across the gap. In the outer part of the bay there are two conspicuous rocks, the Carrickstone off Pulpit Rock and the Gilstone which is covered at high tide. Within the confines of the bay you have mixed bottom which will produce pollack, wrasse, conger and flats with mackerel and garfish in the summer months.

Crow Sound is the area between St.Mary's and the Eastern Isles between a line drawn from Innisidgen to Little Ganinick in the NW to a line from Gap Point on St.Mary's to Trinity Ledge in the south east. Inside the northern boundary the water is very shallow indeed while outside Crow Sound, from Gap Point to Trinity Ledge the average depth is 24 fathoms. This means that one has the whole range of types of bottom at varying depth. The whole area of Crow Sound, clear of the ledges and the rough patches is good for flatfish, being a local inshore trawling mark. Up to four hundred plaice have been taken here in past years by local fishermen in one day's trawling – in the days when you could buy a 'string' of three good plaice for half-a-crown!! The tidal streams within Crow Sound are comparatively weak inside the boundaries already mentioned. It is also sheltered for the most part from the prevailing winds. This side of St.Mary's is often more fishable than any other. It is also less likely to be affected by the long Atlantic swells which can make fishing difficult and indeed dangerous in these waters. When fishing 'The Crow' with the wind between SW and NW do not go too close to the Eastern Isles and thus lose the shelter of St.Mary's.

The Trinity Rock lies on the far side of Crow Sound, half a mile from the SE end of Great Arthur. It is well off-shore from St.Mary's and exposed to wind and tide and should therefore be fished for pollack and coalfish in good conditions. It fishes best for three-quarters of an hour either side of low water. Inside Trinity Rock, on a line with Watermill Bay on St.Mary's there are two other shoal patches, the Ridge Higher Corner and the Ridge Lower Corner. Pollack and coalfish may be caught over the Ridge, also bream. It is best over low water slack and through the early flood tide. One of the best areas for flats is between the Ridge and the Hats Ledges. The navigation buoy marked 'Hats' lies at the southern end of the fairly extensive and in parts extremely shoal area of the Hats Ledges. The shipping channel lies next to the buoy off the end of Innisidgen where the maximum depth is 6½ fathom.

Good plaice have been taken on rod and line around the Hats Buoy; perhaps its mooring chain stirs up the bottom as it swings with the tide and brings them on the feed. Large wrasse up to six pounds have also been taken around these ledges.

Closer inshore on the St.Mary's side, off Watermill, Innisidgen and Pelistry there are two patches of sand which can be safely fished from a small boat under the shelter of the land if the wind is between SW and NW. The patch of sand off Watermill runs right in to the beach. Plaice may be taken here with pollack and wrasse from the weedy edges. Off the back of Toll's Island, about fifty yards from the small 'bay' at the southern end there is a spot appropriately called 'The Mark'. It is well known to the locals as a big wrasse hotspot. It is fished exclusively for wrasse for crabpot bait. It only seems to produce these large fish over the low water slack period. Two rods once had over 100 good wrasse here in one and a half hours fishing over the low water slack period.

The tidal streams around Scilly rotate in a clockwise direction. The rotary offshore streams run towards the islands from a different direction each hour and in passing round or between the islands are affected by the trend of the land, channels and bays and shallow water or shoal areas. In channels and bays the tidal runs will be more noticeable. In a channel the tides are earlier and stronger in the middle. In the case of bays the tide usually ebbs and flows in a circular motion following the contours of the bay rather than straight in and out. When the tide is running strongly over an uneven seabed or where two currents meet it causes a tide race or rip i.e. short steep waves or seas that are forced up in an uneven manner. These can be dangerous to small boats and dinghies. They are particularly dangerous when the tide is running against the wind. Places to watch carefully if fishing from a small dinghy in St.Mary's Sound; between the two bell buoys and Gugh; off Peninnis; off Deep Point and Gap Point across to the Trinity Ledge to the SE of the Eastern Isles, and to a lesser extent off the Creeb when the ebb is flowing against a fresh SW wind. However, occasionally a smooth, narrow passage may exist close inshore between the tide race and the shoreline (as off the Creeb), but great care must be taken if using such a short cut as a safer passage. Scillonian waters can be dangerous for visiting small-boat owners/anglers and local advice should always be sought before going afloat.

Deep Sea Fishing around the Isles of Scilly

Within the islands the water is comparatively shallow and clear with depths not often exceeding nine fathoms. Outside the islands, however, the bottom falls away quite quickly to depths of between twenty and forty fathoms.

Due to its geological structure and its geographical position the Isles of Scilly probably contain more reefs and wrecks per square sea mile than any other coastal sea area around the coast of Britain. Add to this the warming influence of the Gulf Stream and you have what could be the deep sea anglers paradise. Although some south coast charter skippers operating from Plymouth, Mevagissey and Falmouth now offer week-long trips to the Channel Islands and to the Scillies, the waters around the islands are still practically 'virgin waters' for the dedicated deep sea enthusiast.

In this context I would consider 'deep sea angling' to include all waters exceeding a depth of twenty fathoms and all those rocky, shoal areas among the Western Rocks and to the north and east of the islands where an angler would not fish without the services of a licensed boatman from the Isles of Scilly or a professional mainland charter skipper. The wrecks around the islands have proved to be a bonanza for the professional salvage teams working such wrecks as the 'Association' and 'The Colossus' and I am convinced that the other wrecks could provide a wealth of conger, ling, large pollack and coalfish for the deep sea angler.

It would be impossible to mention all the likely wreck and reef marks but a selection might give a taste of what could be achieved in these far south western waters. Although there has been an increase in the number of boats fishing on a commercial basis in Scilly over the past ten years or so there are still plenty of fish available for the visiting charter boat anglers.

Hard Lewis is a ledge, part of which dries to a height of twelve feet at low water, lying to the east of St.Martin's Head. Between Hard Lewis and St.Martin's Head there are depths ranging from 9–22 fathoms. The area fishes best over high water slack and produces pollack and coalfish on feathered traces. Good mackerel are taken here in the summer months, plus specimen wrasse. Off the back of the Eastern Isles ling have been taken on rod and line in excess of 20 lbs.

The point of Samson nearest to the Garrison coast on St.Mary's is known as Southward Wells. To the SSW of Southward Wells lie Great Minalto Ledges and further off a rock which dries out to five feet known as South Well. In this area there are many shoal heads of less than two fathoms, while immediately to the south and east the bottom drops away to eight fathoms. This area fishes best an hour either side and over low water slack. The best recorded rod and line catch in this area totalled 243 pollack to three rods in 2½ hours drift fishing. Off the northern end of Tresco stands a rock called 'The Kettle'. To the NNW of this rock there is Kettle's Bottom which dries eight feet at low water. Very close to this, on the western side, between the Kettle and Shipman Head on Bryher, the depth increases rapidly from sixteen to twenty-five fathoms. This area fishes best for pollack and coalfish on the ebb tide, from half ebb down to low water. Sixty pollack and mackerel were taken here on three rods in just twenty minutes.

Off the south coast of the main island of St.Mary's the twenty fathom line runs close to the shore from Peninnis Head right around to Gap Point. The tide runs strongly here and is especially noticeable when in opposition to the wind. There are two tide runs off the south coast of St.Mary's. It is a good spot to work the tide here for mackerel for bait for bottom fishing for larger species. The rough ground around the Gilstone is good for pollack. Further off shore there is good soft and mixed ground where mainland trawlers in the past have taken as much as 400 stone of quality plaice in one trip. The depth here averages 35 fathoms and offers good general bottom fishing. Best results would probably be taken on the drift, providing conditions were good. Here the slack water periods offer the best opportunity.

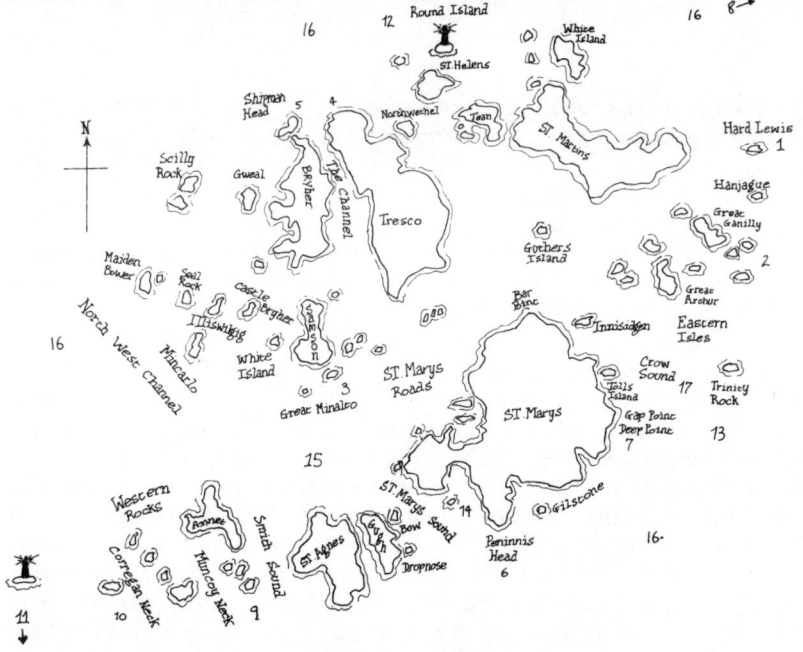

1. Hard Lewis — pollack, coalfish, mackerel and wrasse.
2. Back of the Eastern Isles — ling, tope, cod and whiting.
3. Southward Wells — pollack and coalfish.
4. The Kettle and Kettle's Bottom — pollack and coalfish.
5. Off Shipman Head — pollack, coalfish and blue shark.
6. Twenty fathom line runs close to the shore off Penninnis Head; pollack around the Gilstone; mackerel in the tide run for bait; further off shore to the south for blue shark, plaice, turbot, brill, megrim, cod and whiting as well as tope.
7. Twenty fathom line runs from Penninnis Head to Gap Point close to the shore, offers sheltered, deep water fishing with the wind from the north west.
8. North East of the islands towards the Sevenstone Lightship for conger, ling, tope and bream.
9. Muncoy Neck — pollack and coalfish, conger and ray.
10. Corregan Bight (or Neck) — blonde ray and conger.
11. Pol Bank three miles south of Bishop Rock Lighthouse for ray, ling, conger, skate, also good pollack on shoal ground.
12. Back of Round Island for ray, conger, skate also halibut, ling and tope as well as blue shark taken here.
13. South East of Crow Sound — plaice, turbot, ray, skate, cod and whiting, possibly tope and brill and odd megrim.
14. Outer Porthcressa Bay — rod caught ray and turbot taken here up to 21 lbs weight; also possibility of brill.
15. West of the Steval in St. Mary's Sound, old bream mark on rough ground patches; chance of ray on soft ground.
16. General areas in deep water where blue sharks have been taken on rod and line.
17. Good flatfish ground in Crow Sound, possibility of ray here.

Deep sea angling marks in the Isles of Scilly

Offshore, to the North and East of the Eastern Isles, that is towards the general direction of the Sevenstones Lightship and the mainland of Cornwall, behind Hanjague and Menawethan, the bottom averages out at about 40 fathoms. Here good tope and ling have been taken on rod and line, the ling weighed in at 26 pounds while the tope was just over 30 lbs. At the time of capture both fish featured in a national angling magazine. Mr. Jimmy Williams, former Harbour Master, and Duchy Boatman to H.R.H. the Prince of Wales, landed a fine tope weighing 57 lbs from the area off the Western Rocks, Isles of Scilly.

Among the Western Rocks there are numerous good marks, especially for pollack, coalfish, ray and skate. These waters are among the most dangerous in the whole of the British Isles and should only be fished with an experienced and licensed crew. Muncoy Neck lies at the entrance to Smith Sound and runs north-west between Melledgen and the ledges to the south of Annet. Muncoy Ledges are just to the north-west of Melledgen. Approached from the south the bottom rises from 23 fathoms at the entrance of the Neck to six fathoms across the narrowest part, with shoal patches showing a least depth of two to three fathoms. Mr. Tregear, of St.Mary's, fishing from his own boat, had a catch of over forty pollack here while trolling redgills.

Between Melledgen and Corregan there is Corregan Neck with depths ranging from ten to twenty-seven fathoms. This mark used to be fished by professional long-liners from Cornwall in the autumn for catches of blonde ray. The lines were shot criss-cross fashion across the Neck with catches of 150 stone of ray being taken on six baskets of lines, which would be approximately 800 hooks. My late father's heaviest shot of ray here in one day's fishing was 400 stone of blonde ray with a few conger taken on the hooks nearest the rough ground around the ledges. As the spring tide runs through the neck at about 2½ knots it would appear that slack water would be the best time to fish on rod and line.

The Pol Bank may be classified as a truly deep water mark as it lies approximately three miles south of the Bishop Rock Lighthouse. It rises from a depth of 47 fathoms to a height of 13 fathoms. It is a well known commercial fishing mark and is exploited by mainland fishing boats. It suffers from 'over-falls' when a strong tide is running and can be very dangerous to open boats in rough weather. The ideal for this mark would be a large, well-equipped boat with a professional crew and skipper, flat calm and dead neap tides! Many years ago the old Scillonians would row out to The Pol from St.Mary's and the other off-islands, returning with catches of ray, ling, conger and skate. Further good ground for these species lies to the north of the islands, beyond Round Island where good catches have been taken on long-lines.

Plaice, turbot, ray and skate are also likely to be caught in the deeper water off a line drawn from Gap Point on St.Mary's to Trinity Ledge to the SE of the Eastern Isles, i.e. off the entrance to Crow Sound from the south east. Cod are also taken in the deeper water to the south and east of the islands although they are basically a cold water fish. A cod of 36 pounds stands as a local angling club boat record. Turbot have also been taken by commercial fishermen in the deep water trawling grounds off Peninnis Head. They have also been taken from Melledgen and Corregan Bights among the Western Rocks. Mr. Paddy Daly once took a twenty-pound turbot on rod and line on a mark just off Porthcressa Bay leading to St.Mary's Sound. He also succeeded in boating a fine common skate which weighed over one and a half hundredweight. Mr. Jimmy Williams also landed a large monkfish on rod and line while fishing off Porthcressa Bay on St.Mary's.

John Dory are fairly common in south-western waters although they are usually caught by anglers bottom fishing for other species such as codling and whiting. A likely mark would again be off Peninnis Head. Brill are usually caught on the same ground as turbot and by the same method i.e. drift lining over the soft ground with a flowing mackerel strip or launce bait. Marks worth trying would be off Porthcressa, St.Mary's Sound west of the Steval and the entrance to Crow Sound.

The two species of ray most likely to be caught from Scillonian waters are the blonde ray and the thornback ray, with the painted ray or small-eyed ray being a good runner-up. However, other rays such as the cuckoo ray, sandy ray and spotted ray are all present in south-western waters. Deep water marks are the most likely spots to produce good ray although a blonde ray of 25 pounds was taken in less than five fathoms in Crow Sound. The general area of Crow Sound offers good soft bottom fishing and it is usually a sheltered area when the prevailing wind is between SW and NW.

Although the megrim is not considered a true rod and line specie it is now often taken by rod and line anglers fishing deep water marks for other species. It is caught on the deep water trawling grounds off Peninnis Head and at the entrance to Crow Sound. Although the fish is inferior to turbot and brill it is sold in the fish and chip shops of the south west as 'Megrim Sole.' The Angler Fish, considered by many to be the ugliest fish in British waters, is also caught on soft ground marks where it feeds on the immature flat fish and other species. Years ago hake constituted one of the most important fisheries in the commercial fishing calendar of the South West. Although they are not particularly common in Scillonian waters during the summer months they are taken on a commercial basis by local and foreign vessels working the South Western Approaches. However, hake, like the whiting and the cod do make an appearance into shallower waters during the winter months and are frequently taken by local gill-netters. During the last two winter seasons whiting approaching eight pounds in weight, well in excess of the rod caught record, have been taken by professional fishermen here in the south west corner of the country.

Because they are primarily winter species cod and whiting are not likely to be taken by summer visitors to the islands. They have been taken however to the south of St.Mary's and to the back of the Eastern Isles.

Although the Halibut, the prince of flatfish, is considered to be a northern specie, living exclusively for the benefit of rod and line anglers in the North of Scotland, it has been taken in these waters during the past forty or fifty years or so. Back in the 1920s and 1930s my late father and his brothers worked a local long-liner and landed ten halibut in one week from inshore waters. The best fish weighed ten stone. Their best shot ever consisted of seven halibut in one shot at a controlled price of a guinea a stone. Another halibut was taken on a long-line off Round Island a few years ago. It weighed in at half a hundredweight and was caught by two Scillonian brothers, George and Ronald Symons.

According to the Isles of Scilly Museum Association's publication, 'Fish around the Isles of Scilly', ling are common in deep water away from the islands. Although small ling may be taken from inshore waters when fishing for conger and dogfish, the larger specimens are more likely to be found on the deeper water wreck marks. Ling and conger are taken in commercial quantities by Cornish long-liners fishing to the west of Scilly. Some smaller professional fishermen's craft are now geared to the art of handlining these species over the slack water periods of neap tides. This has resulted in catches of up to 600 stone of ling being landed by a three-man crew over a three day period at sea. Charter boats too are working the wrecks off the south Devon and Cornish coasts and the possibilities of such fishing in Scillonian waters is enormous. As there are numerous wrecks in Scillonian waters I am sure that large conger and ling are there for the taking. Who knows, there may be a new rod-caught record specimen lurking around a Scillonian wreck waiting to be caught by some enterprising angler. Although many wreck marks off the south coast of England are fished as much as thirty miles from port I am sure that good wreck fishing can be found in the waters adjacent to the Isles of Scilly without the angler spending half his time at sea getting to and from the marks. Although skate are caught in these waters there are not any recognised hotspots for them as are found in Irish waters, where good skate are taken in relatively shallow water. However, as the topography of Scilly is in some ways similar to the islands off the coast of south western Ireland there is always the possibility of finding them. The deep water mark of the Pol Bank would be a likely spot.

Tope fishing is a rather specialised form of sea angling and has its own dedicated followers. However, tope have been landed in the islands by 'general' sea anglers fishing off Round Island; off the back of the Eastern Isles and deep off the south shore of St.Mary's, south of Giant's Castle over a patch of mixed ground marked 36 fathoms (r) on the chart.

Shark fishing is another branch of sea angling which I am sure has not been exploited to the full on the Isles of Scilly. It is commonly believed by many visiting anglers that the only port in the British Isles which offers shark fishing is Looe! This is due to the fact that the charter skippers of Looe were the first to exploit this form of fishing and since its early days Looe has become the 'Mecca'. Blue shark, porbeagle and mako have all been taken from the waters around the Cornish coast in recent years with the best blue shark catches being taken off the south coast, while the porbeagles have shown more off the north coast, especially off Padstow. Because of its geographical position it is fair to assume that all these types of shark must pass through Scillonian waters during the course of a season, either passing through to the north or the south of the islands. Although many other Cornish ports such as Falmouth, Penzance and Mousehole offer sharking trips to visiting anglers I am sure that Scilly is much better situated as anglers have less distance to steam before reaching the area where the sharks are likely to be feeding on the mackerel shoals. Boats working from Mount's Bay often have to steam up to and beyond the Wolf Rock Lighthouse before finding their sport. A boat working from Scilly has only to travel three or four miles to the south of St.Mary's to be in a similar situation. Mr. Reggie Phillips of St.Mary's built himself a twin-engined catamaran a few years ago and was able to get to the sharking area to the south of the islands in a mere twenty minutes. Here they took blue sharks up to a maximum of seven feet two inches in length with an estimated weight of approximately 90–100 lbs. Their best bag for a single afternoon session was seventeen blues. Mr. John Poynter of 20 Ennor Close on St.Mary's offers excellent charter fishing facilities on his 35ft diesel catamaran the 'White Hope'. He offers daily shark and angling trips from the harbour on St.Mary's weather permitting. Times are 9.30 to 13.00; 14.00 to 17.30 and 10.00 to 16.30. Shark fishing trips cost £11.00 per head, all gear included while sea angling trips cost £4.50 for a half day trip and £8.00 for a full day trip (see above times). Rods are available on hire at 50p per trip. The 'White Hope' is available for day, evening and winter weekend charter at short notice. For bookings, or details of fishing and other trips, please contact John Poynter, 20 Ennor Close, St.Mary's, telephone Scillonia (0720) 22583. Charter trips may also be arranged by the hour with prices ranging from £7.00 to £7.50 per hour depending on current fuel prices.

Mr. Mike Hicks, a well known Scillonian boatman and a member of the renowned diving teams responsible for the salvage from the wrecks of the 'Association' and the 'Colossus', also experimented with sharking for a couple of seasons with his boat 'Sea King' before he became heavily involved with the salvage business. Many of the Scillonian boatmen are keen fishermen and carry sets of rods for use by their 'paying guests'. Mike Hicks of St.Mary's, who has been operating the 'Sea King' for a number of years, intends bringing a second boat, 'The Gloria' into service for the coming season.

The Former Isles of Scilly Angling Club

Although I formed a Junior Angling Club during my four year stay on St.Mary's the senior club was not formed until 1974. During its short existence the club experienced fluctuating fortunes with membership falling from a maximum of 30 to a hard core of stalwarts, before it folded up completely. The club used the N.F.S.A. Specimen Weight List for Region 'A' (Cornwall) as its own specimen weight list and the club scales carried a valid certificate as required by the N.F.S.A. Complete details of the club and its members catches are held by Mr. Derek Metcalfe, Porthcressa, St.Mary's. The following details of fish recorded during the earlier years of the club were provided by the late Mr. John Ozard of St.Mary's.

Lesser spotted dogfish up to the boat specimen weight of 2-12-0 were regularly taken by boat anglers fishing over soft ground. Red, grey and streaked gurnards were also taken over the same ground. Red Bream were taken up to a weight of about three pounds by charter boat anglers fishing the area around Scilly Rock. Pouting were also taken over rough ground by boat anglers after other species. Catches of blonde ray, small-eyed ray etc were also recorded by club members who fished the area at the back of the Eastern Isles. Blue shark in excess of the specimen weight of 80lbs were also taken to the south of St.Mary's. Mr. Jimmy Williams also landed a rod-caught plaice of 3-12-0 while fishing in Porthcressa Bay. Pollack around the thirteen pounds mark were also taken by club members fishing the area around the Spanish Ledges in St.Mary's Sound.

John Poynter, then of the Atlantic Hotel on St.Mary's, once caught a Bogue which weighed in at over three pounds and would have been a new National Record. He also landed a comparatively rare Rainbow Wrasse which occasionally swims into our south-western waters. This fish weighed 0-10-12 and was sent to the Natural History Museum in London together with the bogue. Another species of wrasse, the rare Goldsinny has also been recorded in the waters around the islands and at the date of capture would have been a British 'mini-record' fish.

Additional Information for the Isles of Scilly

Details of the boat services to the Isles of Scilly are available from the Isles of Scilly Steamship Company Offices at Quay Street,Penzance where the manager Mr. J. Nicholls and his staff are pleased to answer any queries. Phone Penzance 2009. Details of the helicopter service to the Isles of Scilly are available from British Airways at Penzance Heliport, Eastern Green, Penzance (Phone Penzance 3871).

Visitors to the islands are not encouraged to take their cars to Scilly as they are not really necessary. Visitors intending to leave their cars in Penzance are invited to write to the T.I.C., enclosing a s.a.e. for full details of parking and garage facilities. A list of establishments catering for overnight visitors can also be supplied.

Advance bookings are necessary with the Steamship Company and British Airways during the peak holiday season. Any visiting angler contemplating taking his own small craft to the islands on the R.M.V. Scillonian should book well in advance of the proposed date of the visit. Boats will not be carried on busy Saturdays between the end of June and the beginning of September nor over the peak Spring Holiday period. Current freight rates for small craft are as follows:- Boats (including trailer and fitted outboard motor) under 3 metres £29.00 return; 3m but under 4½m £60.00 return; 4½m to 6½m £108 return. Craft over 6½ metres in length are subject to quotation. The length of boats is measured from the towing point of the trailer to the rear extremity of the outboard where fitted (or tailboard). Catamarans are charged 50% extra on the above rates. Outboard motor tanks must be empty and loose cans of petrol are not allowed.

Full information on the Isles of Scilly is available from the T.I.C., Town Hall, Hugh Town, St.Mary's. A brochure with map and accommodation list can be obtained from this address, price 30p.

Details of the St.Mary's Boatmen's Association are also available from the Town Hall while details of fishing trips and pleasure trips are advertised around the harbour area. Details of accommodation on the off-islands and boat operators on each island are also available from the Council Offices on St.Mary's.

Index

Accommodation 57
Additional information – Scilly 60–61
Aire Point 26–29
Anglerfish 19, 24–25, 57
Angling clubs, list of 39–40

Baited spoon 20
Baits 19, 49–50
Bar Beach 49
Bartholomew Buoy 51
Bartholomew Ledge (N) 51
Bartholomew Ledge (S) 51
Bass 13, 15, 19, 20, 25, 28, 29
Bib (or Poor Cod) 14
Bishop Rock Lighthouse 56
Boat proprietors and hirers 38
Bogue 9, 19, 25, 29, 60
Bottom fishing 15
'Bow', The (Scilly) 51
'Bow', The (Sennen) 27, 29
Bream, black 13, 19, 23, 25, 46, 48, 49, 50
Bream, Gilthead 25
Bream, red 13, 19, 23, 24, 25, 46, 48, 49
Brill 13, 19, 28, 29, 49, 57
Brisons, The 26, 27, 30
Brow, The 51
Bryher 45, 46, 54
Bucks, The 23
Bull Huss 19, 25, 48

Camborne 32
Camel, River 20
Camelford 20
Cape Cornwall 26, 27
Carn Base 23
Carn Dhu 23, 25
Carn Morval 50
Carn Near 48
Carn Petrel 23, 25
Carrickstone, The 51
Charter fishing 11, 12, 38, 60, 61
Coalfish 12, 15, 19, 25, 28, 29, 46, 48, 49, 51, 52, 54, 56
Cod 13, 25, 32, 33, 57, 58
Comber 15, 19, 25
Common Topknot 29
Conger 13, 19, 20, 23–25, 29, 46, 48–49, 51, 56, 58
Corkwing wrasse 33
Cornish Division N.F.S.A. 39, 40, 60
Corregan Bight 56
Corregan Neck 56
Coverack 13
Cowloe, The 26, 27, 29
Crabs, soft backed 21, 26

Creagle 27, 28
Creeb, The (Scilly) 53
Crow Sound 52, 57
Cuckoo wrasse 24, 25
Cudden Point 21, 23

Dab 19, 23–25, 28, 30, 46, 48–49
Daymark, The 50
Deep Point 53
District Councils 11, 36
Dogfish, lesser spotted 15, 19, 23–25, 28–29, 46, 48–49, 60
Drethen, The 24, 31
Dropnose 51

Eastern Green, The 21, 23
Eastern Isles 48, 52–54, 56–58, 60
Eel, silver 25
Escalls Carn 27
Estuary fishing, 19, 20

Fal, River 20
Falmouth 12, 13, 15, 53
Fishermen 38
'Flats', The 47
Flounder 15, 19–20, 23–25, 28–29, 31
Flushing 20
Forkbeard, greater 15
Forkbeard, lesser 25
Fowey 12, 15, 20

Gannel, River 20
Gap Point 52–54, 56
Garfish 15, 19, 22, 24–25, 28–29, 46, 48–49, 51
Garrison, The 50–51
Giant's Castle 58
Gillan Creek 20
Gilstone, The 51, 55
Golant 20
Goldsinny 60
Goldsithney SAC 32
Great Arthur 52
Great Minalto Ledges 54
Green Island 51
Gugh 51, 53
Gull Rock 51
Gurnards (various) 19, 23–25, 28–29, 60
Gwenvor 27–28

Haddock 13, 15, 25
Hake 13, 57
Halangy Point 50
Halibut 58
Hanjague 56

Hard Lewis 54
Hats Buoy 52
Hats Ledges 52
Hayle 22
Hayle, River 20
Helford River 20
Helston 32
Herring 25
Hugh Town 51

Innisidgen 52
Isles of Scilly, The 17, 43–61

John Dory 57

Kemyll Rock 23
Kettle, The (Scilly) 54
Kettle's Bottom, (Scilly) 54

Lamorna Cove 21–25
Land's End 13–14, 21, 25, 27, 29, 45
Lariggan Rocks 23
Launce (see Sandeels)
Limpets 46
Ling 13, 15, 19, 23–25, 29, 54, 56, 58
Little Ganinick 52
Lizard, The 12, 21
Logan Rock, The 24
Long Rock 12
Longships Lighthouse 13, 14, 27, 29
Longships Sands 29
Looe 12, 15–17, 59
Lowlee Ledges 23–24
Lugworm 21, 26, 46, 48, 49, 50
Lumpsucker 25

Mackerel 19, 20–22, 24–26, 28–30, 46, 48–51, 54
Mako 59
Malpas 20
Manacles, The 13
Marazion 21, 23
'Mare', The 51
'Mark', The 52
Megrim 33, 57
Melledgen 56
Menawethan 56
Mevagissey 12, 15, 53
Monkfish 57
Mountamopus 23
Mount's Bay 13, 15, 21–25, 27–28, 30–31, 59
Mount's Bay Angling Society 13, 15, 32–35, 37
Mousehole 16, 17, 21–26, 31, 34, 43, 59
Mousehole Island (see St. Clements Island)
Mullet, golden grey 25
Mullet, grey 19, 20, 25, 29
Mullet, grey 19, 20, 25, 29
Mullet, red 25
Muncoy Neck 56

Nanquidno 29
'Neck', The 56
Newford Island 50
Newlyn 21–23, 26–27, 29–30, 32–33
Newquay 15, 16, 20
N.F.S.A. 29, 32, 39, 40, 44, 60
'No Rest' 24
North Rocks, The 28
Nut Rock 46, 51

Old Sawmills 20
Old Town Bay 49, 51
Opah 9, 13, 15, 19

Padstow 15–16, 20, 59
Peal, The 29
Peelers 21, 26
Pelistry 52
Penberth 13
Pendeen Watch 14
Pendrathen 49
Peninnis 53, 54, 57
Penlee 23, 24
Penryn 20
Penzance 13, 14, 16–17, 21–24, 26, 29, 45, 59
Penzer Point 23, 25
Perranuthnoe 23
Pilchard 25
'Pit', The 50
Plaice 19–20, 23–25, 28–29, 31, 46, 48–52, 54, 56, 60
Plymouth 12, 53
'Pol' The 56, 58
'Pol-an-dre' 27, 28, 31
Pollack 12–13, 15, 19–20, 23–25, 28–33, 46, 48–52, 54
Polperro 12, 16
Polruan 20
Porbeagle 15–17, 59
Porthcressa 43, 49, 51, 57, 60
Porthcurno 24
Porth Hellick 19
Porthleven 13, 15, 23, 32
Porthloo 48–49
Porthmellon 49
'Pots', The 51
Pouting 13, 19, 23–25, 48, 60
Prawns 50
Pulpit Rock 51

Ragworm 21, 24, 26, 28, 30–31, 46, 49, 50
Rainbow wrasse 60
Ray (various) 13–15, 19–20, 23, 25, 28–30, 32–34, 46, 56–57, 60
Record fish 15, 32–35
Redruth 32
Reef fishing 11–16
Ridge, Higher Corner 52
Ridger, Lower Corner 52
Rockling, three bearded 19, 25

Rockworm 49, 50
Round Island 56, 58
Runnelstone 13

St. Agnes (Scilly) 45, 46, 51
St. Antony 20
St. Clement's Island 22–23
St. Ives 15, 22
St. Martin's 45–46, 50, 54
St. Martin's Head 54
St. Mary's 43, 45, 46, 48–49, 51–52, 54, 58–61
St. Mary's Harbour 43, 48, 50
St. Mary's Roads 43, 50, 51
St. Mary's Sound 43, 51, 53, 57, 60
St. Mawes 15, 20
St. Michael's Mount 21, 22, 23
Salmon peal 48
Samson 46, 51, 54
Sandeels 20–21, 26, 28, 46, 49, 50, 57
Scad 13, 19, 24–25, 28–29, 32–34, 46, 48–49
Scilly Rock 60
Sennen Cove 21, 25–31
Sevenstones Lightship 56
Shad, allis 25
Shad, twaite 25, 29
Shark, blue 15–17, 59–60
'Shark's Fin' 29
Shark fishing 11–13, 15–17, 59–60
Shrimps 50
Skate 56–58
Smooth-hound 25
Sole 24–25
South'ard Wells 51, 54
Southwell 54
Spanish Ledges 60
Spurdog 13, 15, 19, 23, 49
Star Castle 50
'Stennack', The 24
Steval, The 57
'Stones', The 15

Stony Island 51
Sunfish 25

Tackle shops 37, 38, 39, 50
Tamar, River 20
Tater Dhu 22–24
Taylor's Island 50
Toll's Island 52
Tope 19, 23, 25, 56, 58
Town Beach 49
Trefusis Point 20
Tresco 45, 46, 48, 51, 54
'Tribbens', The 27
Triggerfish 9, 19, 25, 29
Trinity Ledges 52, 53, 56
Trinity Rock 52
Triskey 50
Truro 14, 20
Turbot 13–15, 19, 23, 25, 28–30, 32–33, 35, 46, 49, 56, 57

Useful Information 36–40, 60–61

Vellandreath 28

Wadebridge 20
Watermill 43, 52
Weaver, greater 13, 19, 25, 28, 29
West Penwith 21, 32
Western Rocks 48, 53, 56, 57
Whitesand Bay 26–30
Whiteworm 21, 50
Whiting 13, 15, 19, 24–25, 49, 58
Winkles 46
Wolf Rock Lighthouse 13, 59
Woodcock Ledge 50
Wrasse, various 19, 23–25, 28–29, 31, 46, 49, 51–53
Wreckfish (Stone bass) 9, 16, 19, 25
Wreck fishing 11–13, 15–16, 53–54